INDIAN
FOOD
MADE EASY

Anjum Anand

INDIAN FOOD MADE EASY

Anjum Anand

Photographs by Vanessa Courtier

QUADRILLE

First published in 2007 by
Quadrille Publishing Limited
Alhambra House
27–31 Charing Cross Road
London WC2H 0LS

Reprinted in 2007 (three times)
10 9 8 7 6 5 4

Text © 2007 Anjum Anand
Photographs © 2007 Vanessa Courtier
Design and layout © 2007 Quadrille
Publishing Ltd

Editorial director Anne Furniss
Creative director Helen Lewis
Project editor Gillian Haslam
Designer Lucy Gowans
Photographer Vanessa Courtier
Food styling Susie Theodorou
Props styling Wei Tang
Production Vincent Smith, Ruth Deary

BBC and the BBC logo are trademarks
of the British Broadcasting Corporation
and are used under licence.
BBC logo © BBC 1996

Cataloguing in Publication Data:
a catalogue record for this book is
available from the British Library.

ISBN 978 184400 5710

Printed and bound in Germany

To my dearest
daughter, whose
second full
sentence was
'Mama, what you
cooking?' The
answer, my
darling,
was this.

Contents

Introduction

The unknown can definitely be daunting. I suppose this is why a nation of people who spend as much money as we do on Indian food haven't yet become adept at cooking it.

But as with many challenges in life, once you climb that hill and face those fears, they were never as tough as you imagined and the rewards can be... well, delicious. At least they are in the case of Indian food! And with the fantastic supply of ingredients now available in the supermarkets or at the touch of a button on the internet, there are no more excuses for not cooking something you love to eat. Indian cuisine seems to be surrounded by an aura of mystery and myths, but the truth is anyone can cook it. And that is the aim of this book – to show you just how quick and simple the recipes can be.

Indian cuisine has always been very straightforward – you cooked what grew locally and along with a helping of bread or rice, that was it. It was and still is a regional and seasonal food that has had spices woven into its very DNA as they are considered the elixir of health. It is, at heart, peasant food, eaten as much for taste as it is for nourishment. Meals traditionally consisted of some protein, a vegetable and a staple. The number of dishes served at any one meal did increase with prosperity which, as many lived in joint families with lots of people there to help in the kitchen, was fine.

However, things have changed and people now have less time to devote to culinary tasks. Indian food has always been an integral part of my diet and long ago I felt the need to simplify, streamline and lighten my meals. I really wanted to bring this fantastic, complex and generous cuisine into the twenty-first century. Food is personal, you cook what you want to eat, so cooking an Indian meal can be as easy as baking some fish, grilling some chicken, stir-frying spinach or rustling up some rice and lentils.

The accepted 'wisdom' that Indian food is unhealthy is an unfair allegation. Indian restaurants are not representative of how Indians eat; we don't add cream, ghee or nut pastes to all of our dishes. This cuisine can seem oily but so can the Mediterranean diet, and I think oil is good, when consumed in moderation. And as the cooked accompaniments that required oil were traditionally served in small portions with either boiled rice or simple bread, you would have needed the oil to stay healthy. Most Indians eat well-balanced, nutritious meals incorporating vegetables, lentils, whole grains, dairy and a little meat or fish – all fresh food and fantastic ingredients. What we see as Indian food in this country is often a murky narration of the truth with much lost in translation. The food is, actually, inherently very healthy.

In the UK, Indian food has been on a journey of evolution. We have moved on from inauthentic creamy, fruity curries and can now easily find tandoori and regional options. But there is still so much to discover. India is a country that has so much to offer. It is food that is eaten for breakfast, lunch and dinner. It is everyday food; food for children, adults, friends and family. But every cuisine has all these elements so why has the obvious escaped us for so long? Why has Indian food been relegated to the upper shelves of book stores – the back bench of the United Nations of Cookery and out of most people's reach for so long?

It has been a long road getting here and a slow but exciting journey, but thankfully we can now experience Indian food the way it was intended, at home.

Anjum.

The Indian Kitchen Made Easy

You can make Indian food without having to buy any new cooking equipment but if you like cooking Indian food, or in fact any ethnic meal, there are a few bits and pieces that make the experience easier.

Non-stick karahi

No self-respecting healthy eater would be without non-stick cookware. A karahi is a wok-like pan with a rounded base. The curved bottom allows the food to move easily in the pan without bits of food sticking to and burning in the edge. Once you start to use these pans, you never want to go back to straight-sided saucepans.

Curved cast-iron pan (tava)

We cook most of our flat breads on this shallow, concave cast-iron pan. The pan holds the heat well and the bread cooks quickly and evenly. If you don't have one, a non-stick frying pan will also gets the job done.

Grinders, pestle and mortars, blenders and microplane graters

These are kitchen facilitators. They are not all essentials but I think every self-respecting kitchen should have a blender and microplane grater for making large and small quantities of pastes respectively. Also useful is a pestle and mortar or a small spice grinder for grinding fresh spices.

Muslin cloth

This thin, light cloth is used when making paneer, traditional Indian cheese (see page 26). It is inexpensive and can be washed and reused.

Rolling pin and tongs

The rolling pin is essential for rolling out the many Indian flat breads. Tongs are really useful, not only for turning and handling bread but also to turn vegetables and meats that are grilling in the oven.

Spice container

This is a round steel container – not very attractive but really useful. It houses small deep bowls in which you place all your most used spices so that when you are cooking everything you need is to hand. I actually have two – one for powdered spices and one for whole. This means my cupboards are free of plastic bags of half-used and spilling spices.

Lastly, I cook using gas rather than electricity as I find that I have greater control when cooking and that food cooks quicker on gas. I have explained how the dishes should look and smell at the different stages, so follow these guidelines to get the recipe right as well as following the time guide.

The Recipes Made Easy

Whenever I take things for granted or make assumptions, I get into trouble. So, when it comes to cooking a new cuisine, I assume a lack of knowledge and then look forward to learning about it. When it comes to Indian food, I have seen so many people make preventable mistakes (simple things like choosing the wrong chilli or tomato) that have left their dishes less than perfect. It might be useful to have a quick read of this chapter to ensure the dishes turn out as they should and to start to understand the basics. Also have a look at the glossary on page 156. For those of you who have already mastered the basics and are finding cookbooks repetitive, bear with me as we're still in the early stages in this culinary evolution!

Chillies

People seem to have forgotten that chillies have a wonderful flavour. They can be really hot to eat but are not spicy as such. Remember the basic rule – the bigger the chilli, the milder it is. Green chillies ripen into red ones but have a slightly different flavour. I find the red ones slightly sweeter than the green ones, a bit like capsicums. I often leave chillies whole in my food so that they impart flavour without too much heat as this is mainly contained in the seeds and membranes.

If you don't have fresh chillies, dried red chillies or even chilli flakes are a good substitute; they add heat as well as a little flavour. Chilli powder, however, will give your food a great colour and lots of heat but little flavour. The important thing to remember is that unless a recipe says otherwise, always use the long, thin green chillies that look like knobbly fingers. Other chillies will not give you the same flavour. If you bite into a harsh chilli, follow with yoghurt or something sweet.

Coconut

The coastal regions of the south and west of the country tend to use the ubiquitous coconut to sweeten and to add richness and texture to their dishes. I don't always have a fresh coconut at home so often use canned coconut milk and desiccated coconut instead as they work really well. If, however, you love coconut, buy a coconut grater from a well-stocked Indian shop. They are inexpensive, easy to use and it takes just minutes to grate the nut with little effort.

Garlic

These come in such different sizes, from small and thin to gigantic mutant cloves, so when writing a recipe sometimes indicating how many cloves is not always enough. So, to give you a better indication, one large clove of garlic weighs around 2–2.5g. Yes, I know I'm so pedantic!

Ghee

This is simply clarified butter. It can be bought in stores but is easy to make. Warm unsalted butter in a saucepan and cook gently until the colour changes to pure gold. By this time all the milk impurities will have risen to the surface and should be removed with a spoon. The ghee is now ready to use. Store in a jar in the fridge.

Ginger

People have often asked me where to buy ginger paste, I never realised that people actually bought pastes – they are so easy to make at home. Use a microplane grater or a blender. You can store the paste in teaspoon-sized batches in ice-cube trays in the freezer and add them straight to the pan.

Masala

I often throw the word 'masala' around, assuming everyone knows what I am talking about. I have now realised that, of course, most don't. It is one of the basic foundations of Indian food. It is, in this context, the mixture of ingredients that forms the base of most curries. It is like making a gravy or curry sauce to which you add the main ingredient. A poorly-cooked masala will result in a one-dimensional dish, so take your time and cook the masala properly at each stage. To gauge if it is cooked, look for little bubbles of oil being released on the sides and if still in doubt, try it – if there are no harsh flavours, it is properly cooked.

Meat and Poultry

The best way to get the most from your red or white meat is to cook it on the bone as this provides that wonderful meaty flavour that we often add back in with good-quality stock (which is made from those same bones). We cook our red meat until falling off the bone – there is never any trace of pink – but I leave it to you to cook lamb how you like. If you use meat without the bones, you can either add extra bones to the dish as it cooks and fish them out later, or add some stock instead of water. When cooking lamb, I usually choose shoulder or leg, but you can use cheaper cuts if a recipe requires long, slow cooking. Your butcher will prepare cubed lamb with the bone in if you ask. Also, do skin chicken joints as we do not brown them in the pan and this can leave the cooked skin a little flabby and chewy. It will also act as a barrier, preventing the flavours of the gravy getting into the flesh.

Onions

These are a really important ingredient in Indian food. They add depth of flavour, body, richness and sweetness to a dish. Not all curries will have

onions, but the onion masala (base of a curry/gravy) will always be used abundantly in north Indian restaurant kitchens. When cooking onions, you need to make sure that the onion is properly cooked and to the right stage. As onions cook, they absorb any oil in the pan, then once cooked they release the oil back and you know they are done. If the recipe says the onions should be soft, then they should be translucent; if golden, then the softened onion should be cooked until browned on the sides and turning golden in the centre. Be wary of cooking the onions over too high a heat when they will brown before they soften – check by pressing a piece.

Spices

Whole spices should be the first thing added to the hot oil in a pan. They only take 10–20 seconds to cook and when they release their aroma and just start to darken, quickly add the next ingredient. Powdered spices are very delicate so cook over a low heat. Spices should be kept in airtight containers away from heat and sunlight (see page 8). It's always best to buy whole spices as they keep better and retain more flavour. They take seconds to grind in a spice grinder (see page 8).

To roast spices, use a small frying pan or saucepan and dry roast over a moderate to low heat, shaking the pan often to cook them evenly. You can't leave them unattended as they need to be taken off the heat and poured out of the pan as soon as they are roasted and fragrant, around 1 minute. Use a pestle and mortar to grind to a powder.

Tamarind

This is a coastal fruit that grows in papery brown pods on trees of the same name. It is an important ingredient and is used to add a sour element to many Southern curries. It can be a bit fiddly to extract the paste from the block of tamarind, but ready-made pastes are now available in supermarkets. Add judiciously as they all have different strengths.

Tomatoes

In India tomatoes are used for their slight sourness as well as their flavour. For Indian food, you need to buy the cheap cooking tomatoes – the ones you normally avoid as they look unripe and flavourless. Juicy, sweet plum or vine tomatoes are great for salads and raitas but can sometimes be too sweet for our dishes.

Yoghurt

As yoghurt ages, it gets more and more sour, which is fine as we sometimes need yoghurt for its freshness and other times for its sour quality. Fresh and sweet for desserts and raitas, slightly sour for general cooking and even very sour for some specific dishes; the recipe will always say if it should be particularly fresh or sour. If the yoghurt is too fresh, you may need to add a little lemon juice at the end of the cooking. Taste and decide. The Onken biopot range of yoghurt always seems to work well.

Succulent Chicken Tikka Wraps

Chilli Cheese Toast

Masala Scrambled Eggs

Potato and Pea Samosas

Paneer, Mushroom and Spinach Wraps

Paneer

Simple Semolina Pilaff

LIGHT
MEALS
and
SNACKS

Tandoori Lamb Wraps

Paneer and Vegetable Skewers

Savoury Semolina Cake

Makes 8

500g chicken breast, skinned, boned and cut into 2.5cm cubes
vegetable oil, for frying
10 wooden skewers, soaked in water for 30 minutes
2 tbsp melted butter, to baste
8 tortillas
¾ tsp chaat masala (optional)
½ onion, 2 tomatoes and one head of Little Gem lettuce, all finely sliced
150ml coriander and mint chutney

Marinade

150ml Greek-style thick yoghurt
1 tbsp vegetable oil
8g fresh ginger, peeled
15g garlic (approximately 8 large cloves), peeled
¼ – ½ tsp red chilli powder, or to taste
¾ tsp garam masala
generous pinch of green and black cardamom seeds and fennel seeds, ground together
¾ –1 tsp salt, or to taste
30g Cheddar cheese, coarsely grated
1½ tbsp lemon juice
1 egg
2 rounded tbsp gram flour

Succulent Chicken Tikka Wraps

These easy wraps make a perfect light lunch. Don't let the cheese in the marinade throw you – this is an authentic tandoori recipe. Cheese was first introduced as a way to quieten the flavours of the original chicken tikka for the tourists, the strong flavours being replaced with more delicate spices. The result was so delicious that this has now become a standard tandoori recipe and is found across India. We often make mini versions to serve with pre-dinner drinks, and the chicken is also great served with salad and raita.

Blend together the ingredients for the marinade and tip into a non-metallic bowl. Pierce the chicken all over with a fork and add to the marinade. Leave to marinate in the fridge for a few hours, if possible. Bring back to room temperature before cooking.

Preheat the grill. Brush the grill rack liberally with oil and place some foil below to catch any drips. Thread the chicken pieces onto the skewers, spacing them apart so they do not touch. Grill for 6 minutes (using the upper shelf if your grill has that option), turning halfway, then baste with the butter and grill for another minute – the chicken should be slightly charred at the edges and cooked through.

Meanwhile, wrap the tortillas in foil and warm in the oven for 5 minutes while the chicken is cooking.

Using a fork, slide the chicken pieces off the skewers onto a plate and sprinkle over the chaat masala, if using. Divide the chicken into eight portions and place each in the middle of a warmed tortilla, top with the vegetables and spoon over 1½–2 tablespoons of the chutney. Fold over the top of the tortilla, pull in the sides and continue wrapping. Cut the wrap in half on the diagonal and serve. Repeat with the remaining tortillas and serve.

Serves 6

400g boned lamb, cut into 2cm cubes
and pierced with a fork
10 wooden skewers, soaked in water
for 30 minutes
2 tbsp melted butter, for basting
6 tortillas
sliced onions, lettuce and sliced
tomatoes, to serve
100ml green chutney mixed with 3 tbsp
yoghurt, to serve

Marinade

150ml Greek-style thick yoghurt
$\frac{1}{2}$ small onion, peeled and roughly
chopped
15g garlic (approximately 8 large
cloves), peeled
8g fresh ginger, peeled
1$\frac{1}{2}$ tsp garam masala
1$\frac{1}{2}$ tsp ground cumin
1 tsp ground coriander
$\frac{1}{2}$ tsp fennel seeds, ground
$\frac{1}{4}$ tsp freshly ground black peppercorns
1 tbsp vegetable oil
2 tbsp fresh coriander leaves
$\frac{1}{2}$ tsp red chilli powder, or to taste
2 tsp lemon juice
1 tsp salt, or to taste

Tandoori Lamb Wraps

These wraps are the perfect grab-and-go meal. You can prepare the ingredients well in advance and simply grill the lamb in the time it takes you to slice the tomato and onion. The chutney also keeps well in the fridge for a few days. The flavours are clean and deep and the textures varied. You can also use seasoned yoghurt and some chopped fresh coriander and mint instead of the chutney.

Blend all the marinade ingredients until smooth. Pour into a non-metallic bowl, mix in the lamb and leave to marinate for as long as possible – overnight in the fridge would be best. Bring back to room temperature before cooking.

Preheat the grill. Thread the lamb onto the skewers, leaving a space between each piece, and place under the grill. Cook for 5–6 minutes until tender, turning halfway through cooking. Alternatively, cook in an oven preheated to 200°C/400°F/gas mark 6 for 8 minutes. Baste with the butter and cook another minute or two for slightly pink meat (or for slightly longer if you prefer meat well done).

Wrap the tortillas in foil and warm in the oven for the last 5 minutes of the cooking time.

Divide the lamb into six portions and place in the centre of the warmed tortillas. Top with some of the vegetables and spoon over 1$\frac{1}{2}$ tablespoons of green chutney. Roll and serve.

Serves 5

Marinade

75ml Greek-style thick yoghurt
¾ tsp each garam masala, ground
    cumin, fennel and green cardamom
    powder
2 tsp garlic paste
1 rounded tsp ginger paste
2 tsp gram flour
salt, to taste
2 tsp lemon juice
¼ – ½ tsp red chilli powder, or to taste
2 tsp vegetable oil
2 tbsp water

Spinach paste

225g baby spinach leaves, washed
45g fresh coriander, leaves and stalks
15g garlic (approximately 6 large
    cloves), peeled
15g fresh ginger, peeled and roughly
    chopped
6 tbsp roasted and salted peanuts
2–3 tbsp lemon juice, or to taste
1 tbsp vegetable oil
salt and freshly ground black pepper
1–3 green chillies (optional)

200g portobello mushrooms
6 wooden skewers, soaked in water for
    30 minutes
300–350g paneer, or to taste (see
    page 26), cut into 2.5cm cubes
2 tbsp vegetable oil, for frying, plus
    extra for oiling pan
100ml water
½ small onion, peeled and thinly sliced
5 flour tortillas

Paneer, Mushroom and Spinach Wraps

This vegetarian wrap has enough flavours and textures to please all palates. The tandoori mushrooms add meatiness and depth of flavour and the paneer adds freshness, while the spinach paste brings all the flavours together. If you don't have time to make all the different elements, the wrap works just as well without the mushrooms or without the paneer; the spinach paste is the only essential ingredient.

Clean the mushrooms, then boil them in water for 15 minutes. Drain and leave to cool, then slice thickly.

Blend all the marinade ingredients to a smooth paste and tip into a non-metallic bowl. Add the mushrooms to the marinade and leave for 20 minutes.

Preheat the oven to 200°C/400°F/gas mark 6 and oil a roasting tin. Thread the mushrooms, well-coated in the marinade, onto the skewers and bake in the oven for 20 minutes, turning halfway. Once cooked, add to a bowl with the paneer.

Blend all the ingredients for the spinach paste to a smooth paste. Heat the oil in a large non-stick saucepan or frying pan and add the spinach paste and 100ml water. Cook over a moderate heat for about 15 minutes until it starts to thicken and become smooth and creamy. Add the paneer, mushrooms and onion and cook for another minute or until the onion just starts to wilt.

Meanwhile, wrap the tortillas in foil and warm in the oven for a few minutes. Divide the filling into five portions and wrap each in one of the tortillas. Roll up and cut in half on the diagonal.

Chilli Cheese Toast

Makes 2

100–120g Cheddar cheese or your
    preferred cheese, grated
10g onion, finely chopped
$\frac{1}{2}$ small tomato, finely chopped
$\frac{1}{4}$ tsp finely sliced green chillies
1 tsp finely chopped fresh coriander
2 slices of bread

We all already love cheese on toast but once you start eating this version, it becomes very hard to revert back to the simpler one. Add as much chilli as you want or, if you are really nervous, leave it out completely – it is still the best cheese on toast around.

Preheat the oven to 200°C/400°F/ gas mark 6. Mix together all the ingredients except the bread. Pile the mixture evenly on top of the bread and bake in the oven for a couple of minutes until crisp and browning on the sides. Serve hot.

Opposite: *Chilli Cheese Toast*

Masala Scrambled Eggs

Serves 1

1 tsp vegetable oil
small knob of butter
$\frac{1}{4}$ small onion, peeled and finely
    chopped
2 eggs
$\frac{1}{2}$ small tomato, finely chopped
$\frac{1}{2}$ green chilli, finely sliced
1 heaped tbsp chopped fresh
    coriander
salt, to taste

This is a quick concoction that I eat for breakfast at least twice a week. This simple dish shows that Indian food is not all spices and heat. There are no spices in this dish – just good flavours and a little sliced green chilli for punch. Once you start to eat eggs cooked in this way, it is difficult to enjoy them plain.

Heat the oil and butter in a non-stick frying pan. Add the onion and cook for 2 minutes.

Meanwhile, whisk the eggs with the tomato, chilli, fresh coriander and salt. Add the eggs to the pan and scramble as you would normally, leaving them a little longer than usual.

Simple Semolina Pilaff

Serves 1

1 tbsp vegetable oil
$\frac{1}{3}$ tsp mustard seeds
$\frac{1}{3}$ tsp Bengal gram
3 tbsp chopped onion
$\frac{1}{2}$ green chilli, finely sliced
handful of frozen peas
salt, to taste
50g coarse-grain semolina
8 curry leaves
125ml water

This light and nourishing pilaff, made with semolina rather than rice, is often eaten for breakfast. It is a mild dish that can be eaten by all – I feed it to my young daughter, making it with milk rather than water and omitting the chillies, for a nutritious, calcium-packed dish. You can add more vegetables to this recipe if you wish.

Heat the oil in a non-stick saucepan. Add the mustard seeds and gram and cook until the gram starts to brown. Stir in the onion, chilli, peas and salt and cook until the onions are translucent, then add a splash of water to cook the peas.

When soft, cook off the water. Add the semolina and curry leaves and stir-fry over a high heat for a minute or two or until you can smell their distinctive aroma. Add the water and continue cooking and stirring until it comes together or until you can smell the semolina. Serve hot.

3 tbsp vegetable oil, plus extra for
  oiling
165g semolina
125ml plain yoghurt
125ml water
40g frozen peas
2 tbsp chopped onion
1 small carrot, peeled and grated
handful of frozen or fresh green beans,
  roughly broken up
8g fresh ginger, peeled and pounded
  into a paste
¼ – 1 tsp red chilli powder, or to taste
½ tsp turmeric
salt, to taste (season well)
1 tsp mustard seeds
½ tsp cumin seeds
½ tsp bicarbonate of soda
1 tsp sesame seeds

Savoury Semolina Cake

This savoury cake, known as handvo, is spongy on the inside, crispy on the edges and replete with the textures of a variety of vegetables. It is light, satisfying and easy to make. It hails from the Gujarati community but this is my cheat's version – no soaking or grinding required, so purists beware! Use any vegetables you have – either those listed here or experiment with courgettes, cabbage, spinach or fresh fenugreek leaves.

Preheat the oven to 200°C/400°F/gas mark 6 and oil a large loaf tin.

Mix together the semolina, yoghurt, water, vegetables, ginger, spices and salt to make a batter of a medium-thick consistency. If it is too thick, add a splash of water. Taste and adjust the seasoning if necessary.

Heat the oil in a small saucepan. Add the mustard and cumin seeds and cook for about 20 seconds until the mustard seeds have popped and the cumin is aromatic. Stir into the batter.

Stir in the bicarbonate of soda and immediately pour the mixture into the prepared tin and sprinkle over the sesame seeds. Bake in the preheated oven for 35–40 minutes. The cake is ready when a toothpick inserted into the centre comes out clean and when the edges are crisp. Leave the cake to cool in the tin.

Makes 250g

2 litres full-fat milk
200–250ml fresh yoghurt or 2 tbsp
lemon juice

Paneer

Paneer is home-made, unsalted white cheese. It has all the taste of a fresh farmer's cheese and a dense, crumbly texture that works wonderfully either combined with the spices of India or served simply with flaky sea salt, freshly ground black pepper and a drizzle of good-quality olive oil. Paneer is a good source of protein and is packed with vitamins and minerals. You can now buy it ready-made from the supermarket, but as this recipe shows, it is really easy to make your own. Paneer forms the main ingredient in several dishes in this book (for example, see pages 20, 29 and 98).

Bring the milk to a boil in a heavy-based saucepan. Once the milk starts to boil and rise up, stir in 200ml of the yoghurt or all the lemon juice. Keeping the milk on the heat, stir gently to help the milk curdle – it should only take a minute or so. If it does not separate, add the rest of the yoghurt and keep stirring. The curds will coagulate and separate from the watery whey. Remove from the heat.

Line a large sieve with muslin or cheesecloth and place over a large bowl or saucepan. Pour the cheese into the lined sieve and run some cold water through it. Wrap the cheese in the cloth and hang it from the tap over the sink to allow the excess water to drain for 10 minutes. Then, keeping it fairly tightly wrapped, place on your work surface with a heavy weight on top (I refill the same saucepan with the whey or water and place it on top) for 30–40 minutes or until it is flattened into a firm block. Then cut into cubes or crumble, depending how you want to use it.

Store any unused pieces of paneer in the refrigerator in water in a covered container. You can also freeze it in an airtight container. Defrost thoroughly before use.

Makes 6 skewers

300g paneer (see page 26), cut into
    2.5cm cubes
1 large onion, peeled and cut into
    2.5cm cubes
1 green and 1 red capsicum, cored and
    cut into 2.5cm cubes
vegetable oil, for greasing
6 wooden skewers, soaked in water for
    1 hour
2 tbsp melted butter
chaat masala, to sprinkle

Marinade

125ml Greek-style yoghurt
5g fresh ginger, peeled
10g garlic (approximately 3 large
    cloves), peeled
salt, to taste
$\frac{1}{4}$ – $\frac{1}{2}$ tsp chilli powder, or to taste
1 tsp garam masala
2 tbsp lemon juice, or to taste
2 tbsp vegetable oil
1 tbsp gram flour
1 tsp cumin powder
seeds of 6 green cardamom pods,
    powdered with a pestle and mortar

Paneer and Vegetable Skewers

We will be forever indebted to the north-west of India for the introduction of tandoori food. My father remembers how most homes in his town had their own small tandoor ovens to cook bread in. Now that tandoori-style food is cooked all over the world, the actual tandoor is often incidental and mainly found in restaurants – it is the flavours that we crave, however they are created. This is my vegetarian tandoori recipe. It is full flavoured, has lots of texture and is very satisfying regardless of whether you are a vegetarian or not. Tandoori food is often served with sliced or chopped tomatoes, red onions and cucumbers seasoned and drizzled in lemon juice, and some green chutney (see page 134).

Purée all the marinade ingredients until smooth, then place in a non-metallic bowl. Add the paneer and vegetables and allow them to soak up the flavours for 30–40 minutes or longer in the fridge.

Heat the grill to a high setting and oil a roasting tin liberally. Place a roasting tin or some foil below the grill to catch any drips.

Thread the vegetables and paneer alternately onto the skewers. Grill for 7 minutes, drizzle over the melted butter, turn and cook for another 2–4 minutes or until charred at the edges. Alternatively, cook in an oven preheated to 200°C/400°F/gas mark 6 for 8–10 minutes, turning halfway through. Sprinkle the skewers liberally with chaat masala and serve with bread.

3 tbsp vegetable oil
$\frac{1}{2}$ tsp mustard seeds
60g chopped onion
6g fresh ginger, peeled and finely chopped
60g frozen peas
1 tbsp coriander powder
1 tsp cumin powder
$\frac{1}{4}$ tsp red chilli powder
$\frac{1}{2} - \frac{3}{4}$ tsp garam masala
1–2 tsp dried mango powder, or to taste
salt, to taste
600g potatoes, boiled until soft, peeled
    and crushed into large lumps
4 tbsp chopped fresh coriander leaves
1 packet filo pastry
5 tbsp melted butter, for brushing
2 tbsp sesame seeds (optional; you can
    also use poppy or nigella seeds)

Potato and Pea Samosas

This samosa recipe is simplified by using shop-bought filo pastry, which gives a light and crispy covering, rather than the heavier gram-flour dough traditionally used. The filling is delicious with a mixture of sweet, spicy, tart and buttery flavours in each mouthful. Indian tea-time snacks tend to be vegetarian, but we always have a batch of mini cocktail samosas made with minced lamb in the freezer for unexpected guests, to be served with drinks to whet their appetites. Serve with green or tamarind chutney (see pages 134 and 135).

Heat the oil in a small non-stick saucepan and fry the mustard seeds for about 10 seconds until they splutter. Add the onion and ginger and cook for 2 minutes over a high heat. Add the peas and give the pan a good stir, then add the spices, salt and a splash of water. Cook for 1 minute, then add the potatoes and coriander and cook for 2–3 minutes. Taste and adjust seasoning.

Preheat the oven to 200°C/400°F/gas mark 6. Unroll the pastry, peel off one piece, then cover the remainder with cling film and a damp tea towel to prevent it drying out. Lay the first piece of pastry flat on a clean surface and brush with melted butter. Fold in one third of the pastry lengthways. Brush again with the butter and fold in the other end to make a long triple-layered strip. Halve the strip crosswise – your strip needs to be only about 10cm long.

Place one rounded teaspoon of the filling at one of the short ends of the strip, leaving a 2cm border. Fold the right corner diagonally to the left, enclosing the filling and forming a triangle. Fold again along the upper crease of the triangle. Keep folding this way until you reach the end of the strip. Brush the outer surface with the butter. Place on a baking sheet and cover while you make the rest of the samosas. Before baking, sprinkle with sesame seeds, if using. Bake in the centre of the oven for 30–35 minutes until golden and crisp, turning halfway. Serve with green or tamarind chutney.

Chicken in Creamy **Yoghurt**

Oven-fried **Chilli** Chicken

Goan Coconut Chicken Curry

My Chicken **Korma**

Chicken with **Peppercorns**
and Shredded Ginger

Chicken Burgers

CHICKEN

Green Coriander Chicken

Mangalorean Chicken

Classic Northern Chicken Curry

Serves 6–8

1.3kg chicken, skinned and jointed
   into small pieces
2 tbsp vegetable oil
1 small onion, peeled and chopped
1–2 green chillies, slit (optional)
1 large or 2 small black cardamom pods
handful of fresh coriander stalks and
   leaves, finely chopped

Marinade

15g garlic (approximately 7 large
   cloves), peeled
20g fresh ginger, peeled
400ml plain yoghurt
4 tsp coriander powder
$\frac{1}{2}$–1 tsp red chilli powder
1 rounded tsp garam masala
2 tsp salt, or to taste
$\frac{1}{2}$ tsp cumin powder

Chicken in Creamy Yoghurt

This is a delicious dish whose simplicity belies its full flavour. The recipe has been in my family for as long as I can remember and it has always been a firm favourite of mine. It is easy to cook and can be made with the minimum of spices and even less effort. As a bonus for the health-conscious amongst you, very little oil is used in the dish which simply relies on good-quality chicken and fresh yoghurt for its wonderful depth of flavour and creaminess. I like to serve the chicken with some green vegetables, roti or naan.

Purée the garlic and ginger with some of the yoghurt to make a smooth paste, then stir in the remaining marinade ingredients. Tip into a non-metallic bowl, add the chicken and leave to marinate in the fridge for as long as possible (I leave mine overnight). Bring back to room temperature before cooking.

Pour the chicken and the marinade into a large saucepan and place over a high heat.

Meanwhile, heat the oil in a small pan and fry the onion and chillies, if using, for about 6 minutes or until soft. Once done, add to the chicken along with the cardamom pods and continue cooking over a high heat for about 15–20 minutes until the watery curry becomes creamy and covers only one-third of the chicken.

Cover the pan and cook the chicken over a very low heat for a further 10–15 minutes until it is tender and the gravy is rich and creamy. Stir occasionally, making sure there is enough water in the pan and adding a splash more if necessary. Stir in the coriander, check the seasoning and serve.

Serves 4–6

6 tbsp dessicated coconut
1–2 fresh large red chillies
8g fresh ginger, peeled
15g garlic (approximately 5 large
    cloves), peeled
½ tbsp cumin seeds
1 tsp coriander seeds

2 tsp white poppy seeds
1½ tbsp vegetable oil
1 small-medium onion, peeled and sliced
salt, to taste
1kg chicken, skinned and cut into
    small joints
250ml coconut milk
2 tsp tamarind paste, or to taste
50g creamed coconut

Goan Coconut Chicken Curry

This creamy curry is typical Goan fare. It is a mild dish that is full of flavour. The triple
dose of coconut is not a statement but an easy way of substituting fresh coconut which
can be cumbersome to deal with. In an ideal world, one coconut would be cracked
open, some flesh ground with water to get thick milk, some ground for thin milk and
the remainder grated. I find it easier to substitute three shop-bought alternatives but
you can use the real thing if you prefer. Goans often eat their curries with their local
bread or red, nutty rice. I think it works well with any rice, naan or even baguette.

Dry-roast the coconut in a small pan over a medium heat until it is golden brown. Grind into a fine paste with
the red chillies, ginger, garlic, cumin, coriander and poppy seeds. Add a splash of water to help it grind down.

Heat the oil in a non-stick saucepan. Add the onion and fry for 4–5 minutes until it is golden brown. Add the salt
and paste and fry for another 5–6 minutes or until all the excess moisture has dried off and the paste has had
a few minutes to fry off.

Add the chicken pieces and cook in the paste for 5 minutes over a moderate heat, then stir in the coconut milk
and bring to a gently boil. Turn the heat down to low and cook, covered, for 30–35 minutes or until the chicken
is cooked through.

Uncover the pan and stir in the tamarind and creamed coconut; cook for another few minutes or until the gravy
is creamy. If there is not enough water in the pan at any time, add a splash or two from the kettle.

Serves 6

800g chicken joints, skinned and
    forked all over
3 tbsp vegetable oil
¼ tsp salt
¼ tsp freshly ground black pepper
¾ tsp cumin powder
4 slices of white bread, crumbed
1 large egg, beaten
1 lemon, cut into wedges, to serve

Marinade

10g fresh ginger, peeled and roughly
    chopped
25g garlic (approximately 9 large
    cloves), peeled
2–4 green chillies, seeds and
    membranes removed, if wanted
1 tsp salt, or to taste
1 tsp garam masala
1 tbsp lemon juice
2 tbsp vegetable oil

Oven-fried Chilli Chicken

These delicious joints of chicken are crisp on the outside and juicy on the inside. They are my idea of perfect sharing food, especially if men and TV are involved. The flavours are clean and simple and the cooking process is easy. I like to serve these fresh from the oven, so all I do is throw them in when my friends are having their first drink and they are ready just in time. The green chilli is hot but it is the flavour that is really important here, so scrape out the seeds and cut off the membranes, if you wish, to minimise the heat.

Blend all the marinade ingredients into a paste and place in a non-metallic bowl. Add the chicken and coat well in the paste. Leave in the fridge to marinate for a couple of hours or overnight. Bring back to room temperature before cooking.

Preheat the oven to 225°C/425°F/gas mark 7. Pour the oil into a roasting tin large enough to accommodate the chicken in one open layer. Place the pan on a high shelf in the oven to heat up for 15 minutes.

Mix the salt, black pepper and cumin powder into the breadcrumbs. Take the chicken out of the marinade, letting the excess drip off, and roll in the spicy crumbs, ensuring an even coating on all sides. Dip into the egg and add a second coating of crumbs.

Place the chicken in the oiled roasting tin and cook for 20 minutes. Then lower the oven temperature to 200°C/400°F/gas mark 6, turn the chicken over and cook for another 15–25 minutes (depending on the size of the joints) or until cooked through. Serve with lemon wedges.

Serves 4

700g bone-in small chicken joints,
　　skinned and cleaned
2 tbsp vegetable oil or ghee
10 black peppercorns
10 green cardamom pods
1 black cardamom pod
10 cloves
1 shard of cinnamon
1 piece of mace
1–2 green chillies, left whole
salt and freshly ground black pepper,
　　to taste
1 medium onion, peeled and chopped
200ml water
70g creamed coconut
3 tbsp ground almonds
¾ tsp garam masala
good pinch of sugar
handful of fresh coriander leaves and
　　stalks, chopped

Marinade

200ml plain yoghurt
1 heaped tbsp garlic paste
1 heaped tbsp ginger paste
2 tsp ground coriander

My Chicken Korma

Korma is the name given to any pale, creamy curry. It can be made with yoghurt, cream, nut and seed pastes and coconut – there don't seem to be any rules. To me, korma comes from the tables of the Mogul royalty. It is usually quite rich but more delicate than many other curries. There is normally a little fried and ground coconut added to the dish but, as I wouldn't go to the trouble of extracting the flesh from a coconut for such a small quantity, I opt for creamed coconut. In this recipe I have tried to restrain my use of the heavier dairy products, but if you wish you can replace some of the yoghurt in the marinade with cream. I think this curry is delicious and it's really quick and easy to make.

Mix the marinade ingredients together in a non-metallic bowl, add the chicken, stir and marinate for at least 30 minutes or for as long as possible. Cover and put in the fridge, if you have the time to leave it longer. Bring back to room temperature before cooking.

Heat the oil in a large non-stick pan and add the whole spices, give the pan a good stir and add the onion, green chillies and salt. Fry for about 6 minutes until the onions are golden. Add the chicken along with the marinade and the water. Turn the heat up and bring to the boil, then simmer, covered, over a lowish heat for about 25–35 minutes, depending on the size of the joints, until the chicken is tender, stirring every now and then. Add a splash of water if the pan is getting dry at any stage. Stir in the coconut and almonds, and cook, uncovered, for another 3 minutes until the gravy is creamy.

Add the garam masala, sugar and fresh coriander, taste and adjust seasoning. Serve with rice or roti.

Serves 6

1 tbsp vegetable oil
½ medium onion, peeled and chopped
1kg chicken, skinned and cut into
    small joints
200ml water
salt, to taste
1 tbsp butter
1 tbsp lemon juice, or to taste

Paste

120g fresh coriander stalks
1 medium onion, peeled and quartered
1–2 green chillies, halved
20g garlic (approximately 7 large
    cloves), peeled
12g fresh ginger, peeled
12 black peppercorns
1 tsp coriander seeds
1 tsp cumin seeds
1 tbsp white poppy seeds
2 cloves
1 shard of cinnamon
6 green cardamom pods

Green Coriander Chicken

For me, the colour green, when linked to food, means freshness and herby undernotes. This is a delicious dish where the coriander is used for taste, rather than for fragrance and texture. It is light and summery, and with coriander now growing locally in the UK, you can enjoy it knowing that it is possibly fresh from your local allotment or countryside.

Blend together the ingredients for the paste, reserving 10g of coriander.

Heat the oil in a non-stick saucepan and fry the onion until soft and beginning to brown. Add the paste and cook for 10 minutes, stirring often over a moderate to high heat, adding a splash of water if necessary. Then stir in the chicken, water, salt and butter and bring to a boil. Cover and cook over a low heat until the chicken is cooked, around 25–35 minutes.

Uncover and cook off all the extra water in the pan over a high heat, stirring often. Then adjust the seasoning and stir in the lemon juice. Chop the reserved coriander and stir in. Serve with any flat bread or rice.

4 tbsp vegetable oil
7 cloves
3 shards of cinnamon
7 green cardamom pods
2 small-medium onions, peeled and
    finely chopped
3 tbsp finely chopped fresh ginger
25g garlic (approximately 9 large
    cloves), peeled and finely chopped
salt, to taste
1 tsp turmeric
1 tsp red chilli powder
2 scant tbsp coriander powder
4 medium cooking tomatoes, puréed
900g small chicken or 2 poussins,
    skinned and jointed
700ml water, or more if needed
1 tsp garam masala
handful of fresh coriander leaves

Classic Northern Chicken Curry

To Indians, a curry simply implies a gravied dish. The actual flavours will reflect the region in which you eat it. This recipe is from Punjab and for an Indian this would be enough of a description. We know to expect the robust flavours of onions, tomatoes, ginger, garlic and garam masala. In the old days, when I was still living at home, a night out generally ended with my girlfriends coming back to my place and ransacking the fridge to find leftovers of this curry (for some unknown reason there was always, always some lying around). We would then polish off every last scrap with rounds of hot buttered toast to mop up the flavourful gravy as we meticulously dissected the evening's events as only women can.

Heat the oil in a large non-stick saucepan. Add the whole spices and fry for about 20 seconds until aromatic. Add the onion and cook over a moderate heat for about 10 minutes until a rich golden brown, stirring often.

Stir in the ginger and garlic and cook for a further 40 seconds before adding the salt and powdered spices, stir for a further 10 seconds. Pour in the tomatoes and cook over a moderate heat for about 10 minutes until the liquid in the pan has dried off and the oil leaves the sides of the dry masala.

Add the chicken and brown over moderate to high heat for 3–4 minutes. Add enough water to almost cover the chicken, bring to a boil and then cook over a slow to moderate heat until the chicken is cooked through. The slower it cooks, the better it tastes. This takes about 15–20 minutes for small joints and up to 25–30 minutes for larger ones.

Stir in the garam masala and coriander leaves just before serving.

Makes 4

Burgers

400g chicken mince
6g ginger, peeled and finely chopped
10g garlic (approximately 3 large
 cloves), peeled and finely chopped
1 small onion, peeled, half finely
 chopped (for the burgers) and half
 sliced into rings (for serving)
large handful of fresh coriander leaves
 and stalks, finely chopped
1 heaped tsp salt
¾ tsp garam masala
1½ slices of medium-cut bread, crumbed
1 egg
1 tsp cumin powder
1 tsp lemon juice
1–2 green chillies (optional), chopped
 and seeded
1 tbsp vegetable oil, plus extra for
 oiling the pan

To serve

7 tbsp light mayonnaise
2 tbsp chopped fresh coriander leaves
2 tsp chopped fresh mint leaves
1–2 tsp lemon juice, or to taste
salt, to taste
¼ – ½ tsp black pepper, or to taste
4 burger buns, halved
lettuce leaves, shredded
1 beef tomato, sliced

Chicken Burgers

Whilst a burger is obviously not of Indian origin, small, succulent chicken burger-like kebabs are often served as appetisers with drinks. For a more substantial snack, they are sometimes wrapped in a huge handkerchief-like thin bread with sliced onions, tomatoes and herb chutney. This recipe just involves a different choice of bread, it works beautifully and the flavours are still Indian. You can leave out the chillies when making them for children and stir them in before cooking up a batch for yourselves. Also, some may still want the taste of ketchup instead of the chutney-flavoured mayo.

Mix together all the ingredients for the burgers, leaving out the onion rings. Allow the mixture to rest for 10 minutes in the fridge. Preheat the oven to 200°C/400°F/gas mark 6.

Mould the mince into four burgers and place on an oiled baking sheet. Place in the oven and cook for 10 minutes, turning halfway through the cooking time.

Meanwhile, mix the mayonnaise with the coriander and mint leaves, lemon, salt and pepper. Warm the burger buns in the oven for the final 2 minutes of cooking time.

Place a small handful of the lettuce on the bottom of each bun with the sliced tomato and onion rings and a good dollop of the herbed mayonnaise. Top with the hot burgers and finish off with the top half of the bun.

Serves 4

4 tbsp desiccated coconut
1 tbsp coriander seeds
2 shards of cinnamon
5 cloves
10 black peppercorns
1 tbsp poppy seeds
15g garlic (approximately 5 large
    cloves), peeled
7g fresh ginger, peeled
1 medium onion, peeled and quartered,
    and $\frac{1}{2}$ small onion, peeled and
    chopped
1–3 large fat red chillies, to taste
400ml water
2 tbsp vegetable oil
salt, to taste
700g chicken joints, skinned and
    jointed
3 tomatoes, cut into wedges
handful of fresh coriander stalks
    and leaves

Mangalorean Chicken

This chicken is not as spicy as it looks – rather, it's really well rounded and mild. The coconut reminds you of its coastal provenance and the red chillies are typical of Mangalorean cuisine. They love their food hot! I have given you a range option, so choose whichever suits your eating preferences but be aware that different batches of chillies have different strengths so use judiciously.

Toast the coconut in a dry pan until it is golden. In a bowl, mix together the toasted coconut, coriander seeds, cinnamon, cloves, peppercorns, poppy seeds, garlic, ginger, the quartered onion, red chillies and 150ml of the water to form a paste.

Heat the oil in a non-stick saucepan, add the chopped onion and fry until browned. Add the paste and salt and cook for 10 minutes over a moderate to high heat, adding a splash of water if necessary. Add the chicken and tomatoes and cook until the tomatoes have softened, then add the remaining water. Bring to a boil, then lower the heat and simmer, covered, for 25–35 minutes until the chicken is cooked.

When the chicken is cooked, uncover and reduce the excess water in the pan over a high heat, stirring often. Stir in the coriander and adjust the seasoning before serving.

Serves 6

1kg chicken joints, skinned with all
    visible fat removed
3 tbsp vegetable oil
1 small onion, peeled and finely chopped
1–2 green chillies, to taste
15g fresh ginger, peeled and sliced into
    thin shreds
1 tbsp coriander powder
salt, to taste
200ml water
1 tbsp black peppercorns, coarsely
    ground, or to taste
$\frac{1}{2}$ tsp garam masala
2 tsp lemon juice
2 handfuls of chopped fresh coriander
    leaves and stalks

Marinade

30g garlic (approximately 10 large
    cloves), peeled
10g fresh ginger, peeled
1 tsp garam masala
1 chicken stock cube, dissolved in
    3 tbsp hot water

Chicken with Peppercorns and Shredded Ginger

This dish is one of our family basics and whenever certain friends came over for dinner they hoped, nay, almost asked in advance, for this dish. I soon anticipated the question and made it almost to order. The predominant flavours of this dish are the freshly ground black pepper, plus ginger and coriander. All the other ingredients round off these clean and intense flavours. Really, truly delicious.

Make a paste with the garlic, ginger, garam masala and chicken stock. Tip into a non-metallic bowl, add the chicken, stir to coat well and marinate in the fridge for at least 1 hour or for as long as possible. Return to room temperature before cooking.

Heat the oil in a non-stick saucepan. Add the onion and sauté for about 8 minutes or until brown. Add the green chillies, ginger, coriander powder and salt and cook for 30–40 seconds.

Add the chicken with the marinade and sear on all sides, about 3–4 minutes. Add the water and black pepper and bring to a boil. Then lower the heat, cover and simmer for 20–30 minutes until the chicken is tender. Stir the pan occasionally, adding splashes of hot water if necessary.

Increase the heat and stir the chicken for at least 3–4 minutes to reduce the gravy to just a few tablespoons. Stir in the garam masala, lemon juice and coriander just before serving.

Himalayan Lamb
and Yoghurt Curry

Dry Coconut Lamb

Curried Lamb Meatballs

North Indian
Lamb Curry

Honey-roasted Spicy Leg of Lamb

MEAT

Herby Lamb Chops

Lamb with Squat
Green Chillies

Lamb Burgers with Herbed Yoghurt

Easy All-in-one Lamb Curry

Serves 4–5

2 bay leaves
¾ tsp ground ginger
2 black cardamom pods
2 shards of cinnamon
8 small cloves
10 green cardamom pods
1 piece of mace
¾ tsp salt
12 black peppercorns, lightly pounded
4 good tsp ground fennel seeds
600g cubes of lamb, with the bone in
250ml water
300ml plain yoghurt
2 tbsp oil or ghee
¾ tsp garam masala
salt, to taste

Himalayan Lamb and Yoghurt Curry

This is a really unusual, clean, mild and fragrant curry from Kashmir. It is so different from most people's perception of Indian food that it is worth trying just to understand the diversity of Indian flavour combinations. It is typical of this region in that it has no onions or garlic, and ginger is in powdered form. The flavour is provided entirely by the spices, yoghurt and meat, and for this reason, all should be good quality and the meat should be cooked on the bone as this provides much of the lamb's flavour. As a bonus, there is no chopping and hardly any washing up. Serve with simple boiled rice.

Place the bay leaves, ginger, black cardamom pods, cinnamon, half the cloves, half the green cardamom pods, mace, salt, peppercorns and 3 teaspoons of the ground fennel seeds in a non-stick saucepan along with the meat and the water. Bring to a boil, then cover and cook on a low heat for about 35 minutes until the meat is tender.

Stir in the yoghurt and bring to a gentle simmer, then cook on a low heat for another 10 minutes. Add a splash of boiled water from the kettle if necessary.

Meanwhile, heat the oil or ghee in a small pan and add the remaining cloves and cardamom pods, cook for 20 seconds and stir into the meat with the garam masala and remaining ground fennel seeds. Check the seasoning and serve with plain boiled rice.

The dish has a pale, thin, flavourful and aromatic gravy that is delicious with rice or Indian bread. If the gravy has reduced too much, add a little boiled water from the kettle.

Serves 4

1 medium-large onion, peeled and finely chopped
3 tbsp vegetable oil
2 bay leaves
1 small shard of cinnamon
2½ medium cooking tomatoes
8g fresh ginger, peeled
10g garlic (approximately 3 large cloves), peeled
800ml water
½ tsp turmeric
¼ – ¾ tsp red chilli powder, or to taste
2 tsp coriander powder
1 tsp garam masala
salt, to taste
good handful of fresh coriander stalks and leaves, chopped

Meatballs

400g lamb mince
2 tbsp finely chopped fresh coriander leaves and stalks
¾ tsp garam masala
1 tsp finely chopped ginger
10g garlic (approximately 3 cloves), peeled and finely chopped
1 large egg
½ tsp salt

Curried Lamb Meatballs

This delicious curry with its light, floating meatballs was one of my favourite childhood dishes. It conjures up memories of a pot of bubbling gravy with each bursting bubble releasing the fragrant scent of a well-blended and perfectly cooked masala. This is a great dish for the whole family without the chilli (add a little paprika for colour). Serve with basmati rice or with buttery noodles.

Mix all the ingredients for the meatballs, adding 3 tablespoons of the chopped onion.

Heat the oil in a deep non-stick saucepan. Add the bay leaves, cinnamon shard and remaining chopped onion and fry until the onion is golden brown.

Meanwhile, purée the tomatoes, ginger and garlic and add to the pan. Cook over a medium heat until the oil comes to the surface, about 7–8 minutes, then add 200ml of the water and continue cooking until all the water has evaporated. Stir-fry this paste for 3 minutes, then add the powdered spices and salt. Add the remaining water, cover, bring to a boil and simmer for 5–6 minutes while you form walnut-sized meatballs from the mince.

Add the meatballs to the pan, cover and simmer for 20 minutes, shaking the pan every so often but do not stir as the meatballs can break. Add the coriander, shake the pan and serve.

25g fresh ginger, peeled
30g garlic (approximately 10 large
 cloves), peeled
3 tbsp vegetable oil
2 each black and green cardamom pods
1 bay leaf
1 large onion, peeled and finely chopped
800g small lamb cubes, with bone in
1–2 green chillies, whole (optional)
$\frac{1}{2}$ tsp turmeric powder
1 tbsp coriander powder
1 tsp garam masala
salt, to taste
4 medium tomatoes, puréed
500ml water
good handful of fresh coriander leaves
 and stalks, chopped

North Indian Lamb Curry

This is a typical, warming dish from Punjab and we have been making it at home for as long as I can remember. The whole spices added at the beginning of the recipe bring a wonderful depth and roundness to the flavour of the curry but if you don't have any, don't worry – the curry is delicious regardless. The coriander adds a lightness and freshness to the dish, making it so much more than just a garnish. Eat the lamb with roti or rice pilaff or, as we sometimes did, in a hot, buttered baguette – truly delicious.

Make a paste of the ginger and garlic, adding a little water to help if you are using a blender.

Heat the oil in a large non-stick saucepan. Add the cardamom pods and bay leaf and stir for 10 seconds before adding the onion. Fry for about 8 minutes until nicely browned. Add the lamb and stir-fry for 2–3 minutes, then add the ginger and garlic paste, the spices and salt. Cook, stirring, for a couple of minutes or until the pan is dry.

Add the tomatoes, bring to a boil, and simmer until the masala has cooked through, around 10–15 minutes. The oil will come out of the masala and there should be no harshness to taste. Add the water, bring to a boil, then lower the heat and cook, covered, for 35–45 minutes until the lamb is tender. Stir occasionally and make sure there is always some water in the pan. When cooked, stir in the coriander, turn off the heat and serve.

Serves 4

1½ tbsp vegetable oil
1 medium onion, peeled and sliced
2–4 green chillies, left whole
600g lamb chops, trimmed of any
    excess fat
10g garlic (approximately 3 large
    cloves), peeled and chopped
2 tsp chopped fresh ginger
1 tsp garam masala
salt, to taste
200ml water
110g fresh coriander stalks
4 sprigs of fresh mint, leaves only
4 tbsp plain yoghurt
lemon juice, to taste

Herby Lamb Chops

Lamb chops have masses of flavour and work wonderfully with Indian spices. Also, as we like to eat with our hands, eating fiddly chops actually adds to our eating pleasure. These chops are cooked simply with some basic flavourings, then have a large helping of coriander and mint added to the gravy. These mellow with cooking so the end result is not too herby but very aromatic and flavourful. I do keep a little back to add at the end of the cooking to reintroduce the freshness that will be sacrificed at the altar of flavour.

Heat the oil in a non-stick saucepan and fry the onion until past golden. Add chillies and the lamb chops and brown on both sides, stirring often. Then add the garlic, ginger and garam masala and stir for 30 seconds.

Add the salt and water, bring to a boil, then cover and cook over a low-moderate heat for 15 minutes – the lamb should be cooked by now. Dry off all the excess water in the pan over a high heat, stirring often.

Purée 100g of the coriander with the mint and yoghurt. Stir into the lamb and cook for a further 15 minutes over a moderate heat until there is little gravy remaining. Adjust the seasoning, chop and add the remaining coriander and drizzle with a little lemon juice, if necessary. Serve with flat bread.

Serves 5–6

2.2kg leg of lamb
100g blanched almonds
100ml thick Greek-style yoghurt
1$\frac{1}{2}$ tbsp honey

Marinade

2 tbsp vegetable oil
5 tbsp lemon juice
15g fresh ginger, peeled and roughly chopped
20g garlic (approximately 6 large cloves), peeled and roughly chopped
1 tbsp cumin powder
1 tbsp coriander powder
$\frac{1}{4}$ tsp red chilli powder
1 tbsp garam masala
salt, to taste
$\frac{1}{2}$ tsp freshly ground black pepper
2 tbsp water

Honey-roasted Spicy Leg of Lamb

This leg of lamb is slightly spicy, lemony and at first bite, a little sweet. Honey and lemon make a fantastic combination and the spices just add to it. As with all roast lamb recipes, this dish needs to marinate properly – ideally for 24 hours – and takes some time to cook, but it is, in essence, an easy dish. It is wonderful with simple roasted potatoes and a vegetable.

Blend together all the ingredients for the marinade.

Trim the lamb of the excess fat and membranes. Make deep, regular cuts all over the flesh with a short, sharp knife. Rub in the marinade, making sure you work it into the deep cuts. Place the lamb in a plastic food bag with any remaining marinade and leave in the fridge for 24 hours if possible, or for at least 6–8 hours.

Blend together 70g of the almonds, the yoghurt and half the honey. Rub into the lamb and ideally leave in the fridge for another 2 hours, but even 30 minutes will help. Bring to room temperature before cooking.

Preheat the oven to 225°C/425°F/gas mark 7. Place the lamb on a rack with a roasting tray underneath. Cook for 15 minutes, then lower the heat to 180°C/350°F/gas mark 4. Cook for 20–25 minutes per 500g plus another 15 minutes depending on how pink you like your lamb. Baste the lamb every 20–30 minutes or so with the juices that have dripped into the roasting tray.

Scatter over the remaining almonds and drizzle over the remaining honey and roast for another 10 minutes. If you wish, check the lamb a meat thermometer – you are looking for a temperature of 130–150°C, and the higher the temperature, the more cooked the meat.

Remove the lamb from the oven and allow it to rest for 15 minutes, covered with foil. Pour the gravy into a jug and skim off any excess fat. Carve the meat and serve the gravy on the side.

800g lamb, cut into small pieces with
    the bone in
300ml plain yoghurt
¾ tsp turmeric powder
1 tbsp ginger paste
1 tbsp garlic paste
1 tsp cumin powder
2 tsp coriander powder
1 tsp ground mustard seeds (ideally
    grind them yourself in a spice grinder)
1 heaped tbsp white poppy seeds, made
    into a paste (I use a pestle and
    mortar and a splash of water)
salt, to taste
3 tbsp vegetable oil
1 large onion, peeled and finely chopped
1–2 green chillies, forked once
1 tsp garam masala
½ tsp freshly ground black pepper
good handful of fresh coriander stalks
    and leaves, chopped

Easy All-in-one Lamb Curry

As with any Indian lamb dish where the meat is cooked until tender and falling off the bone, this recipe is a lesson in slow-cooked food, but as the dish almost takes care of itself this isn't a bother. This is a fantastic, full-of-flavour yet mild curry, but for a spicier version add some whole garam masala (see below) to the hot oil before starting. I fork the chillies before adding them to prevent them bursting in the pan.

Mix the lamb with the yoghurt, turmeric, ginger and garlic pastes, cumin, coriander and mustard seed powder, poppy seed paste and salt. Leave to marinate in a non-metallic bowl for as long as possible or at least until you chop and cook the next batch of ingredients.

Heat the oil in a non-stick saucepan, add the onion and green chillies and fry until the onions are brown, around 6–7 minutes. Add the meat and its marinade and stir-fry over a low heat for 3 minutes. Cover and continue to cook over a low heat for 45–50 minutes or until done, giving the pot a gentle stir every now and then. If the pan is running dry, add a splash of water from the kettle.

Once tender, stir in the garam masala and black pepper; check and adjust seasoning. Always make sure there is enough water in the pan for a little gravy by adding extra from the kettle or cook the lamb over a high flame to dry off any excess water. Stir in the coriander and serve.

Whole garam masala: to add a bigger punch, add 1 black cardamom pod, 4 green cardamom pods, 1 shard of cinnamon, 3 cloves and 1 piece of mace.

Makes 6

1 small onion, peeled
12g fresh ginger, peeled
15g garlic (approximately 4 large
    cloves), peeled
20g fresh coriander stalks and leaves
2–3 green chillies, chopped, or ½–1 tsp
    red chilli powder
450g lamb mince (beef mince can also
    be used)
¾ tsp cumin powder
1½ tsp garam masala
1 rounded tsp salt, or to taste
1 large egg
2 slices of thick-cut white bread,
    crumbed, or enough to bind well
2 tbsp vegetable oil, plus extra for oiling

Herbed yoghurt

300ml Greek-style thick yoghurt
30g fresh coriander leaves,
15g fresh mint leaves or 1 tbsp good-
    quality dried mint
1–2 green chillies (optional)
salt, to taste
½–1 tsp freshly ground black pepper

To serve

6 hamburger buns
lettuce leaves
2 plum tomatoes, sliced crosswise
1 onion, peeled and sliced crosswise
    into large rings

Lamb Burgers with Herbed Yoghurt

This recipe may not sound like an overtly Indian dish, and in a way it isn't. However, it is heavily based on the traditional lamb kebabs we've been eating for hundreds of years. This is my way of incorporating the delicious flavours of these kebabs into everyday eating. The succulent burgers are packed with interesting flavours and they work beautifully with the cool herbed yoghurt and the fresh crunch of the vegetables.

Using a hand blender, finely chop the onion, ginger, garlic, coriander and green chillies by pulsing or chop them all by hand. Add to the mince along with the remaining ingredients.

Shape into six burgers and chill for 20 minutes or until you want to eat, taking them out of the fridge 30 minutes before you want to start cooking.

Meanwhile, mix together all the ingredients for the herbed yoghurt and season to taste.

Heat the oven or grill and cook the burgers on a well-oiled grill or baking sheet for 10 minutes, turning them halfway. I like to add the hamburger buns to the oven for 3–4 minutes before I take the burgers out.

Serve in warmed hamburger buns on a bed of lettuce, tomato and onion rings with a good spoonful of the herbed yoghurt on the top.

100g desiccated coconut
3 tbsp vegetable oil
2 small onions, peeled and finely sliced
1 tbsp ginger paste
1 tbsp garlic paste
$\frac{1}{2}$ tsp turmeric
$\frac{1}{2}$ tsp red chilli powder
4 medium cooking tomatoes, chopped
salt, to taste
900g lamb, cut into 2.5cm pieces with
    the bone in
400ml water
1 tsp garam masala

Dry Coconut Lamb

This really easy lamb dish is not a curry as the fantastic, textured gravy is thick enough to cling to the tender meat. This dish has a depth of sweetness from the onion and the coconut, but is balanced out with the tartness from the tomatoes. Perfect with roti or naan. Leaving the meat on the bone adds flavour – you can ask your butcher to prepare the meat for you.

Dry roast the coconut in a non-stick pan until a little past golden. Reserve.

Heat the oil in a non-stick saucepan, add the onions and cook over a moderate heat until they are well browned. Add the ginger and garlic pastes and the turmeric and chilli powder; cook for about 30 seconds, adding a splash of water from the kettle if the pan is too dry. Add the tomatoes and salt and cook until they have broken down and the oil leaves the sides of the masala, around 10–15 minutes.

Add the lamb and brown over a moderate heat for a few minutes. Add the water, bring to a boil, then cover and simmer over a low heat for 40–50 minutes until the lamb is cooked through. If the pan is running dry at any time, add a splash of water from the kettle. Once cooked, uncover and dry off any excess water over a high heat, stirring often.

When there is only a little liquid left, stir in the garam masala. Check and adjust seasoning, then stir in the roasted coconut and serve.

Serves 6	Marinade
800g lamb, cut into small cubes with the bone in	1 tsp turmeric
3 tbsp vegetable oil	1 tsp fennel seed powder
1 tsp cumin seeds	1 tsp garam masala
½ tsp nigella seeds	1 tbsp white poppy seeds
500ml water	salt, to taste
5–8 fat, short green chillies, slit and seeds removed	10g garlic (about 3 large cloves), peeled
2–3 tsp tamarind paste	15g fresh ginger, peeled and roughly chopped
2 handfuls of fresh coriander leaves and stalks, chopped	1 large onion, peeled and chopped
	2 medium cooking tomatoes

Lamb with Squat Green Chillies

This is a robust dish inspired by the fare of the southern city of Hyderabad. It is spicy, bold, full of flavour and unapologetic. The cuisine from this region is generally sophisticated and its cooks were traditionally considered among the most talented. The fat chillies are full of that inimitable green chilli flavour but without the killer bite of the smaller ones.

Blend the ingredients for the marinade until smooth and pour into a non-metallic bowl. Add the lamb, stir and leave to marinate for as long as possible.

Heat 2 tablespoons of the oil, add the cumin and nigella seeds and fry for about 30 seconds until the cumin browns. Pour in the meat and its marinade and stir-fry over a moderate heat until the masala is cooked, around 12–14 minutes. Taste – it should have no harsh elements. Add the water and bring to a boil, then lower the heat, cover and cook until the lamb is tender, around 35–40 minutes. Keep checking the pot for water and give it a good stir from time to time.

Halfway through cooking the lamb, heat the remaining oil in a small pan and gently fry the chillies for 2 minutes, stirring often. Pour into the cooking meat.

Once the lamb is cooked, uncover and stir in the tamarind paste. Taste and adjust the seasoning, add water from the kettle or dry off any excess – you are looking for a curry that is neither watery nor dry but creamy. Stir in the coriander and serve with naan or rice.

Tandoori Monkfish

Coconut Mackerel Curry

Spiced Crab Cakes with Tamarind Mayonnaise

Simple North Indian Fish Curry

Coconut and Chilli

Pan-fried Halibut

Green Fish Curry

Prawn Balchao

Bengali Prawns

in a Mild Coconut Gravy

FISH
and
SEAFOOD

Mussels with Dry Coconut

Bengali-style Baked Fish

Mangalorean Prawn Curry
with Rice Dumplings

Tandoori Prawns flavoured with Mustard

Serves 4 as a light meal

750g monkfish, cut into large cubes
4 wooden skewers, soaked in water
    for 1 hour
1–2 tbsp melted butter, to baste
lemon wedges, to serve

Marinade

2 tbsp gram flour
4 tbsp Greek-style thick yoghurt
1 tsp lemon juice
½ tsp each carom seeds, turmeric
    powder, red chilli powder and
    paprika
2 tsp ginger paste
1 tbsp garlic paste
1 tsp garam masala
1 tbsp vegetable oil
1 egg
salt, to taste

Tandoori Monkfish

This is a delicious, summery dish that is perfect for serving in warmer weather, although it is eaten all year round in India as bite-size appetisers served with drinks. I think this makes a perfect light meal and when served with a light salad (such as the Herb and Peanut-dressed Spinach Salad on page 102), it is simple and satisfying, yet sophisticated enough to serve to any dinner guest. I have used monkfish here as it is a hearty, meaty fish which goes wonderfully with these flavours, but any firm-fleshed fish would work well.

Mix together all the ingredients for the marinade. Rub well into the fish and leave to marinate in a non-metallic bowl in the fridge for a few hours. Bring back to room temperature before cooking.

Preheat the oven to 180°C/350°F/gas mark 4. Thread the fish onto the skewers, place on a baking sheet and bake for 15 minutes in the middle of the oven. Meanwhile, make the salad and dressing. Then baste the fish with the butter, place the baking sheet on a higher shelf and cook for another 3–4 minutes. Serve with lemon wedges and salad.

3 tbsp vegetable oil
$^1\!/_2$ tsp fenugreek seeds
1 tsp cumin seeds
25 curry leaves, torn
2 medium onions, peeled and roughly
    chopped
2 medium tomatoes, roughly chopped
15g garlic (approximately 5 large
    cloves), peeled and roughly chopped
8g fresh ginger, peeled and roughly
    chopped
1 tsp turmeric
$^3\!/_4$–$1^1\!/_2$ tsp red chilli powder
1 tbsp coriander powder
350ml water
450–500g whole mackerel, cleaned
    and cut into steaks 2.5cm thick
3–5 green chillies, left whole
$1^1\!/_2$ tsp tamarind paste, or to taste
250ml coconut milk
salt, to taste

Coconut Mackerel Curry

This is a gorgeous curry from Chennai, full of flavours that are then tamed by the coconut. It is a coastal dish and proud of it. Mackerel is very popular in the south of India and is used regularly in coconut curries with tamarind to balance the flavours. Cut it into steaks as these keep the fish together and the bones add flavour to the gravy. Serve with rice – nothing else is needed.

Heat the oil in a large non-stick saucepan. Add the fenugreek, cumin seeds and 10 of the curry leaves and fry for 10 seconds. Add the onions and cook for about 6–8 minutes until golden.

Meanwhile, purée together the tomatoes, garlic and ginger and powdered spices. Add to the pan and cook for 8–10 minutes over a high heat or until you can see little droplets of oil on the sides of the masala. Add a splash lof water at any point, if necessary.

Add the water, bring to a boil and then add the fish, green chillies and remaining curry leaves. Bring back to the boil and cook for 3–4 minutes. Stir in most of the tamarind paste but leave a little to add later. Once the fish is cooked, add the coconut milk. Stir well, taste and adjust the seasoning and sourness (adding the remainder of the tamarind paste if necessary) and add more water if you prefer a thinner curry.

Serves 4

3 tbsp vegetable oil
¼ tsp fenugreek seeds
4 medium cooking tomatoes, puréed
¾ tsp turmeric
½ – ¾ tsp red chilli powder, or to taste
½ tsp garam masala
2 handfuls of fresh coriander stalks
      and leaves, roughly chopped
600g any firm white fish steaks
400ml water

Masala

25g garlic (approximately 9 large
      cloves), peeled
4g fresh ginger, peeled
¾ tsp cumin powder
½ tsp black pepper
½ tsp mustard seeds, ground
1 tbsp coriander powder
salt, to taste
40ml water

Simple North Indian Fish Curry

This curry is full-flavoured, tangy and spicy – a curry made for Indians. It is unadulterated and unapologetic. Those who like their Indian food mild need not bother with this dish. It isn't that it is too hot but it is fisherman's food straight from the village, with no onions to sweeten it and no cream or coconut to tame it. The ultimate, authentic peasant food.

Blend the masala ingredients together to make a fine paste.

Heat the oil in a large saucepan and fry the fenugreek seeds for 10 seconds. Add the paste and cook over a moderate heat for 8 minutes or until the oil starts to leave the sides of the pan. Add the tomatoes, turmeric, chilli, garam masala and coriander and cook for 8–10 minutes or until the oil starts to bubble at the sides of the paste. Taste – there should be no harsh elements to the masala.

Add the fish to the pan, coat in the paste and leave on the heat for 3 minutes, then add the water and bring to a boil. Cover and cook over a low heat for about 7 minutes or until the fish is cooked through.

2 tbsp vegetable oil
$\frac{1}{2}$ tsp brown mustard seeds
4 cloves
6 green cardamom pods
1 large shard of cinnamon
1 small onion, peeled, half finely
    chopped and half uncut
10g fresh ginger, peeled and quartered
5g garlic (approximately 2 large
    cloves), peeled
1 tsp coriander powder
300ml coconut milk
2–4 green chillies, left whole
salt, to taste
$\frac{1}{2}$–1 tsp black pepper
$\frac{3}{4}$ tsp garam masala
100ml water
10 curry leaves
500g salmon or firm white fish fillets,
    cut crosswise into large pieces
2–3 tsp lemon juice
50g fresh coriander leaves and stalks,
    chopped

Green Fish Curry

This fish curry is delicate of colour and flavour but absolutely beautiful. The whole spices and green chillies add background flavour but are not strong (the seeds and membranes contain the heat and are not exposed to the curry). You can use almost any firm-fleshed fish – I love it with salmon and the pale peach and green colours are a picture on a plate. Mild enough for children to enjoy.

Heat the oil in a non-stick pan, add the whole spices and cook for 20 seconds. Add the chopped onion and fry for about 4–5 minutes until soft.

Meanwhile, blend together the remaining uncut onion, the ginger, garlic, coriander powder and 100ml of the coconut milk to a smooth purée. Add to the pan with the whole green chillies and salt and cook, covered, for 12–15 minutes, giving the pot an occasional stir.

Stir in the remaining coconut milk and spices, water, curry leaves and fish. Leave to cook undisturbed for about 3–5 minutes, depending on the thickness of the fish.

Gently stir in the lemon juice and the coriander. Check the seasoning and serve with rice.

Serves 4

3½ – 4½ tbsp vegetable oil
1 small onion, peeled and finely chopped
10g fresh ginger, peeled and finely
    chopped
5g garlic (approximately 2 small
    cloves), peeled and finely chopped
2 tsp coriander powder
¼ – ½ tsp red chilli powder
salt, to taste
1 tsp garam masala
2 tbsp lemon juice
25g fresh coriander leaves and stalks,
    chopped
400g prepared crab meat
1 large egg
2½ tbsp mayonnaise
9–10 pieces of thick bread, crumbed
lightly-dressed soft salad leaves, to serve

Tamarind mayonnaise

80g mayonnaise
50ml milk
salt, to taste
¼ tsp freshly ground black pepper
1 scant tbsp tamarind paste, or to taste
handful of fresh coriander leaves and
    stalks, chopped

Spiced Crab Cakes
with Tamarind Mayonnaise

These crab cakes are one of the few fusion dishes in my repertoire. They are absolutely divine, even served simply with a drizzle of lemon, but the peppery tamarind mayonnaise complements them wonderfully and a lightly dressed salad makes it a lovely lunch. Add tamarind to taste as different brands have varying levels of tartness, or use lemon juice and rind which do the same job. The cakes are crisp but melting on the inside, so they have to be turned carefully. The tamarind mayo is rich, so a little goes a long way (you can use light mayo if you prefer).

Preheat the oven to 170°C/350°F/gas mark 4.

Heat 1½ tablespoons of the oil in a pan and fry the onion for about 4 minutes until soft. Add the ginger and garlic and cook for another 40 seconds. Stir in the coriander powder, red chilli powder, salt and garam masala and cook for another 20 seconds, then take off the heat. Add the lemon juice, fresh coriander, crab, egg and mayonnaise. Stir well and add the breadcrumbs. Divide into eight portions and form into round cakes.

Heat 1 tablespoon of oil in a pan and cook the crab cakes in batches, depending how big your pan is, over a low-moderate heat, for about 2 minutes on each side until golden. Place them on a baking tray in the oven to keep warm while you cook the rest. Add the remaining oil when cooking the second batch of cakes.

To make the tamarind mayonnaise, simply whisk all the ingredients together, taste and adjust seasoning. Serve the crab cakes with a spoon of the mayo with salad leaves on the side.

2 halibut steaks or other firm white fish
2 heaped tbsp desiccated coconut
2 heaped tbsp flour
$1\frac{1}{2}$ tbsp vegetable oil
$\frac{1}{2}$ lemon, to serve

Marinade

$\frac{3}{4}$–1 large fat red chilli, seeded and
   roughly chopped
10g fresh ginger, peeled and roughly
   chopped
10g garlic (approximately 3 large
   cloves), peeled and roughly chopped
2 tsp white wine vinegar
2 tsp coriander powder
8 fenugreek seeds
salt, to taste
$\frac{1}{4}$ tsp freshly ground black pepper
1 tsp vegetable oil

Coconut and Chilli Pan-fried Halibut

This delicious recipe is my own version of the traditional Keralan way of frying fish. It works beautifully with any firm white-fleshed fish, so find out what is fresh at your local fishmongers. The dish isn't as spicy as it might first appear as the cooking mellows the flavours and they form only a thin coating on the fish. Really easy to make and perfect for a summer's day, I like to serve this fish with the Chopped Salad with Coconut and Peanuts (see page 103) which is an evocative combination of the flavours of the same coastline.

Pound or blend together the marinade ingredients to make a fine purée. Over-season the mixture slightly as it will be absorbed by the fish. Place the fish in the marinade in a non-metallic bowl and leave for at least 30 minutes.

Mix together the coconut and the flour. Maintaining a generous coating of the purée, coat both sides of the fish steaks well in the dry mixture.

Heat the oil in a large non-stick saucepan and, when hot, add the fish. Cook on a low heat without moving the fish for 4 minutes, then turn over and cook on the other side for a further 3–4 minutes or until done. Squeeze some lemon juice over the fish and serve hot with a salad.

Serves 2

1 tbsp white poppy seeds
1 tsp mustard seeds
2 heaped tbsp plain yoghurt
6g fresh ginger, peeled and chopped
$\frac{1}{2}$–1 green chilli, chopped
salt, to taste
good pinch of black pepper
1 tsp coriander powder
15g fresh coriander stalks and leaves,
    chopped (a good handful)
2 pieces of white-fleshed fillets, such
    as haddock or sole
vegetable oil
10g butter
lemon juice, to taste

Bengali-style Baked Fish

Bengali food is quite unique and different from all other Indian regional cuisine. Here cooks use subtle flavours but are generous with their use of eye-watering mustard, both the oil and seeds. They cherish their fresh seafood and their cuisine is almost a homage to the slippery creatures. This Bengali-style recipe is a delicious example of their food, but I've simplified and mellowed it a little. I love this dish – it takes just minutes to prepare, the same to cook and tastes wonderful. Serve with fresh vegetables or with the Warm Corn, Coconut and Watercress salad on page 99.

Preheat the oven to 190°C/375°F/gas mark 5.

Make a paste of the poppy seeds, mustard seeds, yoghurt, ginger and chilli. I use a pestle and mortar but you can also use a blender. Stir in the salt, pepper, coriander powder and fresh coriander. Taste and adjust the seasoning.

Place the fish in a well-oiled roasting tin. Coat the top of the fish with a good layer of the paste and dot with the butter. Cook for 7–10 minutes or until tender (it depends on the type of fish and the thickness). Drizzle with lemon juice and serve.

Serves 4–6

Dumplings

100g rice flour
½ tsp salt
80–90ml warm water
20g creamed coconut, grated

Curry

1 tsp cumin seeds
2 tsp coriander seeds
9 black peppercorns
¾ tsp mustard seeds
¾ tsp turmeric powder
good pinch of carom seeds
1–2 tsp red chilli powder or to taste
15g garlic (approximately 5 large
    cloves), peeled
1 large onion, peeled, one half roughly
    chopped and the other finely
    chopped
80g creamed coconut, broken up
600ml water
2 tbsp vegetable or coconut oil
1½–2 tsp tamarind paste
salt, to taste
400g prawns, shelled but with the tail
    left intact and cleaned

Mangalorean Prawn Curry with Rice Dumplings

This is a delectable, vibrant curry from the south west coast of India, a region dominated by fresh seafood, coconuts, bright red chillies and a love of spices. This dish would usually only be cooked on special occasions as the rice for the dumplings would require overnight soaking, drying during the day and then grinding by hand, but we are fortunate to be able to buy ground rice. These dumplings have a subtle flavour and texture that go really well with the curry. You can, however, omit them and serve the curry with rice if you wish.

For the dumplings, mix all the ingredients in a bowl until you have soft, pliable dough. Divide and roll into 12 balls or into any shape you like – I like to squeeze them in my palm to make some indentations which catch pools of curry in them. Steam for 12 minutes and set aside.

Meanwhile, start the curry. Place all the spices, garlic, the roughly chopped onion, coconut and 200ml of the water in a blender and blend until very smooth.

Heat the oil in a non-stick pan and fry the remaining onion until light brown. Add the spice paste and cook over a medium heat until the water has dried up, then continue cooking the paste for 6–7 minutes, stirring regularly.

Add the remaining water, tamarind and salt to taste and bring to a boil. Cook over a moderate heat for 10 minutes. Taste and adjust the salt and tamarind paste. Add the prawns and simmer over a low heat for 3–4 minutes. Add the dumplings and simmer for another minute or until the prawns are cooked and the dumplings warmed through.

8g fresh ginger, peeled
15g garlic (approximately 4 large
    cloves), peeled
1–5 dried, mild red chillies (depending
    on your tolerance and the quality of
    chillies)
2 cloves
6 peppercorns
1 tsp cumin seeds
½ tbsp brown mustard seeds
½ tsp turmeric
2½ tbsp vegetable oil
1 small onion, peeled and finely chopped
2 medium tomatoes, finely chopped
1 green chilli, left whole
3–4 tbsp malt or red wine vinegar, or
    to taste
1 tsp sugar
salt, to taste
350g small raw prawns, shelled and
    cleaned

Prawn Balchao

This Goan dish is spicy, tangy and full of flavour. It is how those living on the southern coast take advantage of the fresh, seasonal and cheap prawns that come their way before the monsoons set in and their supply runs dry. They buy baskets of the small prawns and use them to make this pickle, which lasts them through the 'dry' season and into the following year. A little goes a long way as it is spicy but very moreish and is an accompaniment rather than a main dish. If you want to use it as a pickle and keep it for a while, fry the prawns before adding them to the masala paste so there is no more moisture left in them. The gravy is moist and clings to the prawns as an envelope of flavour.

Make a paste of the ginger, garlic, red chillies and all the spices, using a little water until you achieve a fine paste.

Heat the oil in a large non-stick saucepan and fry the onion until golden brown. Add the tomatoes and green chilli and fry for about 10–12 minutes over a moderate to high heat until the mixture becomes a deep burgundy colour. Add a splash of water whenever the pan runs dry.

Add the spice paste and fry for about 5 minutes until the oil leaves the masala. Add the vinegar, sugar and a good amount of salt. Cook for another minute and taste for the balance of flavours. Adjust as you like.

Add the prawns and cook for about 2 minutes until done. To keep as a pickle, store in sterilised jars in the fridge.

Serves 4

16 large king prawns, shelled but with
    the tail left intact, deveined and
    cleaned
4 wooden skewers, soaked in water for
    30 minutes
1 tbsp melted butter, for basting
½ lemon
1 tsp chaat masala
lettuce leaves, lime halves, sliced
    tomato, red onion and green
    chutney, to serve

Marinade

175ml Greek-style yoghurt, strained
2 tbsp ground mustard seeds
1 tsp malt or white wine vinegar
5g fresh ginger, peeled
10g garlic (approximately 3 large
    cloves), peeled
pinch of turmeric
½ tsp red chilli powder
2 tbsp mustard oil or any mild oil
¼ tsp garam masala
salt, to taste

Tandoori Prawns flavoured with Mustard

These tandoori prawns are succulent and indulgent, but manage to remain quite light and healthy. They are the perfect summer barbecue food for friends, but work just as well as a starter or a light meal with a salad. We serve these all year round with a little green chutney as a pre-dinner appetiser with drinks, to whet the appetite and awaken the taste-buds.

Purée the marinade ingredients together with a hand blender until smooth. Place the prawns in the marinade in a non-metallic bowl and leave for 30 minutes, if possible.

Preheat the oven to 200°C/400°F/gas mark 6. Oil a baking sheet.

Slide the prawns onto the skewers and place on the baking sheet. Bake in the oven for 4 minutes. Baste with butter and cook for another 1–2 minutes or until the prawns are done.

Drizzle over a little lemon juice and sprinkle with the chaat masala. Serve on a bed of lettuce with some lime halves, sliced tomato and red onion and some green chutney on the side.

2 medium onions, peeled and cut
    into chunks
8g fresh ginger, peeled and cut
    into chunks
4 cloves
6 green cardamom pods
2 large shards of cinnamon
3 tbsp vegetable oil
5g garlic (approximately 2 large cloves),
    peeled and made into a paste
3–6 green chillies, slit lengthwise
    but left whole
¾ tsp turmeric
1 rounded tsp coriander powder
350–400ml coconut milk
salt, to taste
1 tsp sugar, or to taste
600g medium–large tiger prawns,
    shelled but with the tail left intact,
    deveined and cleaned
50g coconut cream (optional)

Bengali Prawns in a Mild Coconut Gravy

I love this dish. It has the heat and pungency of the green chillies but the actual spices provide the background flavours and are quite mild. It is a hugely popular dish from Bengal, based on the beautiful local tiger prawns. I use both coconut milk and cream as this dish has a rich coconut flavour that would normally be derived from grating and extracting thick and thin milks from fresh coconuts. However, for speed, I cheat and use shop-bought versions. If you wish, you can add a little extra milk and omit the cream altogether.

Blend the onions with the ginger to a fine paste. Grind together 2 cloves, 3 cardamom pods and 1 cinnamon shard in a pestle and mortar; set aside.

Heat the oil in a large non-stick pan, add the remaining whole spices and fry for 20 seconds or until fragrant. Add the onion paste and fry over a low heat, stirring frequently, for 8–10 minutes until golden brown. It is important that the onions are cooked through.

Add the garlic, chillies, turmeric, coriander powder and a splash of water and cook for 1 minute. Stir in the coconut milk, salt and sugar, bring to a boil, then simmer over a low heat for 3–4 minutes. Add the prawns and simmer for 2–3 minutes until cooked,. Stir in the reserved ground spices and coconut cream, if using, and serve.

3 tbsp vegetable oil
1 small onion, peeled and finely chopped
2–4 green chillies, left whole
15g garlic (approximately 4 large
    cloves), peeled and made into a
    paste
10g fresh ginger, peeled and made into
    a paste
salt, to taste
3 tomatoes, chopped into large dice
1kg mussels, scrubbed under water and
    de-bearded; discard any that are
    already open
$\frac{1}{2}$ tsp turmeric powder
1 tbsp garam masala
70g desiccated coconut
handful of fresh coriander leaves and
    stalks, chopped

Mussels with Dry Coconut

This coastal dish from the south-western state of Maharashtra is quick and easy to make and really delicious. I always consider mussels a summery ingredient, but only because I always ate them under the sun, by the sea and on holiday. The flavours of this recipe are well rounded – the tartness from the tomatoes contrasts wonderfully with the sweetness provided by the coconut and mussels, while the various spices add a good background flavour. I serve this dish with some of the mussels in their shells and others taken out and stirred in to the curry, making an appetising and dramatic plate. The masala should be thick enough to coat the mussels and get into any shells.

Heat the oil in a medium non-stick pan and fry the onion until golden brown. Add the chillies, garlic and ginger pastes, salt and stir well for 20 seconds. Add the tomatoes and cook for about 8 minutes, until they have softened and start to break down.

Meanwhile, cook the mussels in a large pot of boiling water until they have opened, around 3 minutes. Remove them with a slotted spoon and set aside. Reserve the water. Discard any mussels that have not opened.

Add the turmeric, garam masala and coconut to the onion mixture and mix well. Then stir in the cooked mussels – some on and some off their shell works best. Add a good splash of the cooking water and stir through. Stir in the coriander and serve with chapatti, naan or even a hunk of bread.

Southern Indian Mixed Vegetable Dish

Smashed-fried Potatoes

Five-seed
Potatoes   Stir-fried Spring Onions

Spinach with Tomatoes

Chopped Salad with Coconut and Peanuts

Sweetcorn Cob Curry

Okra
Fried Spiced

Herb and Peanut-dressed
Spinach Salad

Paneer with Spinach

VEGETABLES

Stuffed Jalapeno
Chillies in Yoghurt

Warm Corn, Coconut and Watercress

Stir-fried Nigella Cabbage

Bengali-style Aubergine
cooked in Yoghurt

Serves 6

50g desiccated coconut
2 $\frac{1}{2}$ tbsp vegetable oil
1 tsp cumin seeds
$\frac{1}{2}$ medium onion, peeled and sliced
1–2 green chillies, slit lengthwise but
    left whole
$\frac{1}{4}$ tsp turmeric
salt, to taste
2 medium potatoes, peeled and cut
    into quarters lengthwise and then
    sliced crosswise on the diagonal
2 medium carrots, peeled and cut into
    fat batons

15cm piece of cucumber, halved
    lengthwise, seeds scooped out and
    cut crosswise into 1cm pieces
100g green beans, topped and tailed
    and sliced lengthwise on the
    diagonal into three
50g shallots, peeled and halved
10g fresh ginger, peeled and roughly
    chopped
2 handfuls of frozen peas
12 curry leaves
5 level tbsp plain yoghurt (fresh, not
    sour)
1 tbsp coconut oil (optional)

Southern Indian Mixed Vegetable Dish

Known as avial, this recipe is one of the most famous vegetable dishes from Tamil Nadu, one of India's southernmost states. And, as such, it has all the elements of the south with the exception of the choice of fresh vegetables, which I have tampered with to circumvent your search for yam, drumsticks and green bananas – all delicious but slightly inaccessible. You can pair it with any seasonal vegetables, although it does need something starchy. The dish is often served at feasts, but I have reduced the amount of oil and coconut used and happily eat it for lunch with some rice or as part of a meal. It is a deceptively easy dish to make and all the work is in the preparation of the vegetables.

Soak the coconut in water to cover while you prepare the vegetables.

Heat the oil in a large non-stick pan. Add the cumin, onion and chillies and sauté for about 4–5 minutes until the onions are soft and colouring. Add the turmeric, salt, potatoes and carrots and cook for 14 minutes, covered, over a low heat. Stir frequently to make sure the vegetables don't catch on the base of the pan, adding a sprinkle of water if necessary. Add the cucumber and beans and continue cooking in the same manner until the vegetables are all tender, a further 6–7 minutes or so.

Meanwhile, blend together the shallots, ginger and coconut, along with its soaking water, to make a fine paste. Add to the pan with the peas and cook, stirring often, for 5 minutes. Tear the curry leaves to release their aroma and add to the pan, give it a good stir and add the yoghurt. Turn off the heat and mix well, pouring over the coconut oil, if using.

vegetable oil, for frying
600g medium-sized red-skinned potatoes,
    peeled and halved lengthwise
salt, to taste
$\frac{1}{2}$ tsp dried mango powder
$\frac{1}{4}$ – $\frac{1}{2}$ tsp red chilli powder
$\frac{1}{2}$ tsp coriander powder

Smashed-fried Potatoes

I very rarely deep-fry anything as I think there are other ways of enjoying the same ingredient in a healthier way. However, these unusual potatoes really are worth enjoying in their pure, unadulterated state. They hail from the Sindhi community and are really quick and fun to make. They are a fantastic accompaniment to barbecues, burgers and any outdoor meals. The dish works best with smallish, red-skinned potatoes as they don't break up when pressed. Alternatively, you can fry up large potato wedges and toss them in the spices.

Heat vegetable oil to a depth of 7.5cm in a wide saucepan or wok. Toss the potatoes with a little salt to season and add to the oil. Fry over a low heat for about 15 minutes, turning occasionally, until they are soft in the centre when tested with the point of a sharp knife. They will still be pale in colour.

Remove from the oil with a slotted spoon and leave to drain on a plate lined with kitchen paper for 5 minutes. Then, using your fingers, lightly flatten the potatoes.

To serve, reheat the oil in the pan, add the flattened potatoes and fry them over a low heat for about 5–6 minutes until they are golden and crisp. Remove and drain on kitchen paper once again and sprinkle a little of each of the spices over the top. Check seasoning and add extra, if necessary. Top each potato with a drop or two of oil to set the powdery spices and serve.

Serves 4–5

500g small new potatoes
3 tbsp vegetable oil
2 tsp panch phoran (also known as
    Bengali 5-Seed Blend)
$\frac{3}{4}$ tsp turmeric powder
salt, to taste
$\frac{1}{4}$ – $\frac{1}{2}$ tsp red chilli powder or 1–2 dried
    red chillies
handful of fresh coriander leaves and
    stalks, chopped

Five-seed Potatoes

These simple and delicious potatoes require little more than a handful of ingredients yet are good enough to serve to your most distinguished friends. Panch phoran is a blend of cumin, fennel, mustard, nigella and fenugreek seeds and it provides a fantastic yet complex flavour and a nuttiness that goes beautifully with the potatoes. I use small new potatoes as I think they look more natural and beautiful than cubes of potatoes, but there is no real difference when it comes to taste so use whichever is easier for you.

Boil the potatoes until just soft, then cool slightly and peel.

Place the oil and seeds in a large saucepan and heat gently so the oil can absorb the flavours of the seeds. Then allow them to fry over a low heat for 20 seconds and add the turmeric, salt and chilli powder or dried chillies. Give the pan a good stir, add the potatoes and coat evenly in the spices. Cook over a low heat, stirring just occasionally, for 3–4 minutes.

Turn up the heat and do not stir the potatoes, allowing them to form a nice crust on their base, then stir and allow to brown on the other side. Once the potatoes have browned a little all over, take the pan off the heat and serve garnished with the coriander.

Serves 4

8 large, fat green chillies
1 medium-large potato, boiled, skin
   removed and mashed
2 tbsp vegetable oil, plus an extra 1 tsp
1 tsp mustard seeds
¾ tsp cumin seeds
½ tsp large fennel seeds
2–3 tbsp water
2½ tbsp dessicated coconut
7 tbsp yoghurt
salt, to taste
15 curry leaves

Stuffing

¼ tsp turmeric
½ tsp ground cumin
½–1 tsp lemon juice, to taste
1 tbsp chopped onion, softened in 2 tsp
   vegetable oil (optional)
salt, to taste

Stuffed Jalapeno Chillies in Yoghurt

There are so many varieties of chillies in India, and indeed here on our doorstep, that it is often difficult to know which ones to use when and how hot they are once cooked. The general rule is the smaller they are, the hotter they are. Most supermarkets now sell these large, fat green chillies which are ideal for stuffing. If using jalapenos, try to find large ones as the stuffing takes away from the heat, as does the yoghurt. It might seem like a complicated dish but it is really easy, just with many components.

Blanch the chillies in boiling salted water for 2 minutes, then drain on kitchen paper. Slit the chillies on the straightest side to make a pocket. Scoop out the seeds and membranes and discard.

Add the stuffing ingredients to the mashed potato and mix together well. Stuff the chillies with just enough mixture to fill.

Heat 2 tablespoons of the oil in a large frying pan. Add ½ teaspoon each of the mustard and cumin seeds and, when they pop, add the fennel seeds. Cook for another 20 seconds, then add the chillies. Sauté over a low heat until they have softened but not lost their shape, about 7–9 minutes.

Meanwhile, whisk the water and coconut into the yoghurt and season. Heat the remaining oil in a small pan and add the remaining mustard and cumin seeds and the curry leaves. Cook for 20–30 seconds and stir into the yoghurt. Leave to cool while the chillies finish cooking.

To serve, place the chillies on a plate and pour over the cool yoghurt.

2–3 tbsp vegetable oil
1 tsp cumin seeds
4 medium cooking tomatoes, puréed
1 rounded tsp coriander powder
$\frac{1}{2}$ tsp turmeric
$\frac{1}{4}$ – $\frac{1}{2}$ tsp red chilli powder
$\frac{1}{4}$ tsp garam masala
salt, to taste
500g baby spinach leaves

Spinach with Tomatoes

Spinach is one of the nation's favourite vegetables. I think the main reasons for this are that it is quick to cook, easy to find and really good for you. Indians tend to overcook their spinach, thereby sacrificing a lot of its freshness and nutrition. Like many of my generation, I want to retain the goodness that comes with these leafy beauties, so I have created this simple, fresh and delicious spinach dish that ticks all the boxes that spinach should. This recipe can be made with less oil if you are being careful, but the oil does round off the sharpness that can accompany spinach.

Heat the oil in a non-stick pan. Add the cumin seeds and fry for about 20 seconds, until aromatic. Add the puréed tomatoes, coriander, turmeric, chilli powder and garam masala as well as salt to taste. Cook for about 6–7 minutes or until you can see oil bubbling on the sides of the tomatoes. Taste to check that the rawness of the tomatoes has gone. Add the spinach, stir and cook for about 5–7 minutes or until well wilted and most of the excess water has dried off, then serve.

Serves 2–3

1 tbsp mustard or vegetable oil
small pinch of asafoetida
$\frac{1}{2}$ tsp brown mustard seeds
$\frac{1}{2}$ tsp nigella seeds
1–2 small dried red chillies, left whole
1 tsp skinned, split black gram lentils
    (urad dal), washed
1 heaped tbsp peanuts, chopped
10–15 curry leaves, torn in half
$\frac{1}{2}$ white cabbage, finely shredded
salt, to taste

Stir-fried Nigella Cabbage

I think this easy recipe is one the best ways to cook cabbage, and the dish can be eaten as a hot salad, a snack or part of a meal. The strong, peppery flavours are enhanced by the mustard oil, although you can also use good old vegetable oil if that's what you have to hand in the kitchen. If you prefer a milder dish, you can omit the chillies, although they do provide extra flavour. Raw peanuts are the best ones to use, but if you only have roasted ones, add them in towards the end of cooking, just to heat them through.

Heat the oil in a large wok or non-stick saucepan. Add the asafoetida and the mustard and nigella seeds and fry for 30 seconds or until they pop. Add the chillies, lentils and peanuts. Turn the heat down and fry until the lentils start to colour, then add the curry leaves, cabbage and salt to taste.

Stir-fry for 3 minutes, then cover the pan and cook on a low heat for a further 6–7 minutes or until the cabbage has wilted but still retains some bite.

Serves 4–5

750g baby spinach leaves, washed
3 tbsp vegetable oil
1 tsp cumin seeds
1 large onion, peeled and chopped
15g fresh ginger, peeled and sliced
    into long julienne
1½ tbsp chopped garlic
1–2 green chillies, left whole
2 tsp coriander powder
salt, to taste
2 litres milk, made into around 250g
    paneer with fresh yoghurt (see
    page 26)
½–1 tsp garam masala, depending
    on quality
6 tbsp full-fat milk or 4 tbsp double cream
1–2 tsp lemon juice, or to taste

Paneer with Spinach

This is a wonderful velvet-like dish with large, fresh cubes of paneer. I don't add much chilli as the green ones are used more for flavour than heat – I like this dish quite mild and creamy. The only spices are cumin, coriander and garam masala and that is just enough for a good background flavour and aroma. I use the double cream when I have friends over, but add the milk when it is just the family. It is probably an Indian thing of serving your guests the best ingredients, even if it's not the healthiest option – I leave it to you. Delicious with simple pilaff or naan.

Blanch the spinach leaves in hot water for 3 minutes or until well wilted. Drain into a colander and run under cold water until they cool. Blend to a smooth paste and set aside.

Heat the oil in a large non-stick pan. Add the cumin seeds and fry for about 30 seconds until fragrant. Add the onion and fry over a mild heat for about 6 minutes or until soft. Add the ginger, garlic and chillies and cook for 1 minute. Add the coriander powder and salt to taste. Cook for another 30 seconds, then add the spinach and a splash of water if necessary. The mixture should be loose but not watery. Bring to a boil and simmer for 3 minutes.

Add the paneer cubes, garam masala and milk or cream. Stir and cook for a few minutes or until the spinach is creamy. Before serving, stir in the lemon juice to taste.

Stir-fried Spring Onions

Serves 4

1 tbsp vegetable oil
$\frac{1}{2}$ tsp cumin seeds
$\frac{1}{2}$ tsp turmeric powder
1 tsp coriander powder
pinch of red chilli powder
bunch of spring onions, preferably
    thin ones, washed and sliced into
    small rounds, around 5–7.5mm long
salt, to taste

This is the quickest side dish you can make. It makes a punchy accompaniment to any dish, even plain layered breads. It is not a full vegetable dish but adds a burst of flavour, colour and texture to anything within minutes.

Heat the oil in a small non-stick saucepan. Add the cumin seeds and fry until lightly coloured and fragrant. Add the rest of the spices, stir-fry for just 5–10 seconds, then add the spring onions. Turn the heat up and stir-fry for 1 minute – they should still remain crunchy. Taste and adjust the seasoning and serve straightaway.

Sweetcorn Cob Curry

Serves 6

1 medium onion, peeled and cut into
    large pieces
3 small cooking tomatoes, quartered
15g fresh ginger, peeled, roughly chopped
10g garlic (approximately 3 large
    cloves), peeled and halved
4 tbsp vegetable oil
1 tsp cumin seeds
$\frac{3}{4}$ tsp turmeric powder
$\frac{1}{2}$–1 tsp chilli powder, or to taste
2 tsp coriander powder
salt, to taste
1kg frozen sweetcorn cobs, defrosted
450ml milk
2 tbsp tomato purée
4 tbsp plain yoghurt
$\frac{1}{2}$ tsp garam masala

This store-cupboard recipe comes from my husband's family. They are from Rajasthan, a northern desert state that produces few fresh vegetables.

Blend together the onion, tomatoes, ginger and garlic to a fine paste.

Heat the oil in a large non-stick pan and fry the cumin seeds for 30 seconds or until aromatic. Add the paste and cook, stirring often, over a moderate-high heat for 10 minutes or until the oil bubbles on the side of the pan.

Add the turmeric, chilli, coriander and salt and stir for 1 minute. Add the corn and cook for 5 minutes. Add the milk and tomato purée, bring to a boil and simmer for 15 minutes or until the whole curry comes together and no longer looks watery. Stir in the yoghurt and garam masala and serve.

Warm Corn, Coconut and Watercress

Serves 3–4

1 tbsp butter
1 tsp vegetable oil
1 tsp mustard seeds
12 curry leaves
1 tsp chopped ginger
1–2 small dry red chillies (optional)
350g frozen or canned sweetcorn,
    drained and washed
250ml milk
salt, to taste
2 tbsp flaked coconut (or desiccated if
    you don't have flaked)
handful of watercress, washed
1 tsp lemon juice, or to taste

This is a warm dish that is almost a salad. The sweetness of the corn, texture of the coconut, warm spices and piquant watercress taste sensational. Watercress is more British than Indian, but we have our fair share of peppery leaves that we often add to our salads.

Heat the butter and oil in a small, non-stick saucepan and add the mustard seeds. Cook for a few seconds, covering the pan once they start to pop. Add the curry leaves, ginger and chillies and give the pan a good stir. Add the corn and milk; cook over a moderate heat for 12–15 minutes until there is little moisture left in the pan.

To serve, season and stir in the coconut, watercress and lemon juice to taste.

Serves 4–6

400g okra, wiped clean with damp
    kitchen paper, topped and tailed
4 tbsp gram flour
vegetable oil, for frying
1 tsp chaat masala
¼ tsp salt
¼ tsp red chilli powder
¼ tsp dried mango powder

Fried Spiced Okra

These crispy, fried shards of okra are so much better in the flesh than they might appear on paper. Whenever I have made this dish, there have never, ever been any leftovers. The gram flour on the okra helps them to crisp up beautifully and the spices add all the flavour they need. Chaat masala is a blend of spices (see page 156) and is the key flavouring in this dish, but having said that, if you don't have any and prefer a simpler dish, give the recipe a go anyway as this is the best way to cook okra. They need to be cooked when you want to eat them as they do not reheat well.

Slice the okra pieces lengthwise into quarters. If they are quite large, slice them again. Toss with the gram flour.

Heat the oil to a moderate-high heat in a large saucepan. Add all or half the okra, depending on the size of your pan. Fry for about 8 minutes, stirring occasionally, until the okra becomes crispy, with some just turning a rich golden brown colour.

Turn the okra onto a plate lined with kitchen paper to drain, then tip into a bowl with the chaat masala, salt, chilli and dried mango powder and toss well together. Serve hot.

Serves 2

3 handfuls of baby spinach leaves
½ shallot, peeled and sliced
1 tomato, sliced into thin wedges

Dressing

2 heaped tbsp roasted peanuts
20g fresh coriander, leaves and
    stalks
10g fresh mint leaves
salt, to taste
¼ tsp cumin
⅛ tsp garlic paste
⅛ tsp ginger paste
2–3 tsp lemon juice, or to taste
3–4 tbsp vegetable oil, such as
    groundnut oil

Herb and Peanut-dressed Spinach Salad

I love salads and although in India we use different salad ingredients and don't often make a dressing, salads are always present on a well-laid Indian table to provide extra crunch to a meal. They are generally dressed with a squeeze of lemon juice and a light sprinkling of salt and chilli powder. This spinach salad is slightly different and is great with any meal, but it's really designed to be served alongside tandoori dishes.

Blend together all the ingredients for the dressing until well mixed. Lightly toss the spinach leaves, sliced shallot and tomato in the dressing and serve.

Serves 2–4

1 tomato, finely chopped
4 tbsp finely chopped cucumber
1 green chilli, finely chopped (optional)
2 tbsp finely chopped onion
handful of fresh coriander leaves and
    stalks, chopped
salt, to taste
2 heaped tbsp desiccated coconut
3 tbsp salted peanuts, roughly chopped
$\frac{1}{4}$ tsp ginger paste
1 tsp vegetable oil
$\frac{1}{4}$ tsp mustard seeds
1 sprig of curry leaves, leaves only
1 tbsp lemon juice, or to taste

Chopped Salad with Coconut and Peanuts

This simple salad is ideal served with a south Indian meal or as an accompaniment to any chicken or fish dish. It is a perfect summer salad with different textures and clean, subtle flavours. I love raw onions, but if you find them a hard to digest leave them out and add more cucumber instead. In typical Indian style, I prefer not to add a proper dressing but simply flavour the salad with mustard seeds and curry leaves.

Mix together the tomato, cucumber, green chilli, onion, coriander, salt, coconut, peanuts and ginger paste.

Heat the oil in a small saucepan. Add the mustard seeds and once they splutter. add the curry leaves and remove from the heat. Add the lemon juice and stir into the salad. Taste and adjust the seasoning.

Serves 4–5

400g small Japanese-style aubergines,
 thinly sliced into rounds
good pinch of turmeric
salt, to taste
¼ tsp red chilli powder
2 tbsp vegetable oil
250ml plain yoghurt
1–1½ tsp sugar
1 rounded tsp cumin seeds, roasted
 and ground
large handful of fresh coriander leaves
 and stalks, chopped

Bengali-style Aubergine cooked in Yoghurt

The first time I tried Bengali food was in a small, family-run restaurant that is a local treasure. In amongst this elaborate introduction to the region's food was this simple, modest accompaniment. I loved it immediately – it is a mild and creamy but confident and versatile dish. I have since tasted many variations, but when I make it at home I always end up recreating those original flavours. Aubergine is such an under-used vegetable but so delicious and goes well with lamb, chicken, fish, lentils and most vegetables. This dish is perfect with Indian breads or even with some fresh baguette.

Coat the aubergines in the turmeric, salt and half the red chilli powder and fry in the oil in a large, non-stick frying pan until soft and the point of a knife goes through with no resistance. You may have to do this in two batches. Drain on a plate lined with kitchen paper and set aside.

Beat 200ml of the yoghurt with the sugar, salt to taste and the remaining red chilli powder and add to a small saucepan. Heat, stirring, over a low heat until warm – this takes a good 5 minutes. Stir in the ground cumin seeds and the aubergine and coriander. Cook for another minute. Turn off the heat and stir in the remaining yoghurt. Check the seasoning and serve.

Toasted
Spiced Chickpeas

Slightly Sweet Bengal
Gram Lentil Curry

Broad Bean Thoran

Buttery Black Lentils

LENTILS
and
BEANS

Garlic and Chilli
Split Pigeon Pea Curry

Simple Spinach
and Lentil Curry

240g whole black lentils, picked
    through, washed and soaked for
    at least 3 hours
1 litre water
10g garlic (approximately 3 large
    cloves), peeled
15g fresh ginger, peeled and halved
    lengthways
180g can of tomato purée
$\frac{1}{2}$–1 tsp red chilli powder
2 green chillies, left whole
salt, to taste
30g butter
$\frac{1}{2}$ onion, peeled and chopped
50ml single cream
1 tsp garam masala
handful of fresh coriander, to garnish

Buttery Black Lentils

For an Indian, this dish is king of the lentil curries and is perhaps the most popular lentil dish in any Indian restaurant. Known as makhni dal, it is a rich, creamy and flavourful curry that everyone seems to love. These lentils take a long time to cook and can be quite heavy to digest, so this is a dish we eat sparingly and on special occasions, which adds to its enjoyment. The lentils would traditionally be cooked overnight over the barest flame so they cook evenly and perfectly, but they are well worth the wait. They are perfect with naan and raita and not much else is needed.

Drain the lentils, discarding their soaking water, and put in a large saucepan with the fresh water. Bring to a boil and then simmer, covered, for about 1 hour or until tender.

Meanwhile, make a paste of the garlic and half the ginger. Finely slice the remaining ginger into long, fine shreds.

When the lentils are tender, add the tomato purée, chilli powder, green chillies, salt and the garlic-ginger paste to the pan. Stir well and cook for another 30 minutes. Keep an eye on the pan and give it an occasional stir as the lentils have a tendency to settle on the base.

Heat the butter in a pan over a low heat, add the onion and sliced ginger and cook for about 4–5 minutes until coloured. Stir into the lentils along with the single cream and garam masala. Cook for a further minute and serve garnished with fresh coriander.

Serves 2–3

2 tbsp vegetable oil
1 tsp cumin seeds
½ tsp turmeric powder
¼ – ¾ tsp red chilli powder
1¼ tbsp coriander powder
1 tsp dried mango powder
¾ tsp garam masala
400g can of chickpeas, drained
    and rinsed
salt, to taste
2 tbsp boiled water
handful of fresh coriander, chopped

Toasted Spiced Chickpeas

This dish is almost instantaneous yet manages to taste great and be healthy. The chickpeas are full of minerals and good fibre and always go down a treat. Ideally, you would eat this dish with Indian layered bread (parathas), but it also works well with naan or even toast. It is great generously stuffed into a warmed pitta with a little dressed salad and green chutney. It is also a good dish to have in your repertoire as it can be thrown together when you have a vegetarian coming over for dinner and have to make an extra dish in a hurry.

Heat the oil in a non-stick saucepan. Add the cumin seeds and fry for about 30–40 seconds or until they give off their aroma and start to darken. Add the remaining spices and salt and cook for 10 seconds. Add the chickpeas and stir to coat well in the spices. Cook for 2 minutes, then add the water and the coriander leaves. Cook for a further minute and serve.

150g skinned and split yellow mung
   lentils
900ml water
8g fresh ginger, peeled and cut into
   thin strips
3 green chillies, left whole (optional)
¾ tsp turmeric powder
2 small tomatoes, puréed
200g baby spinach leaves
salt, to taste
1½ tbsp ghee, butter or vegetable oil
1 tsp cumin seeds
5g garlic (approximately 2 cloves),
   peeled and cut into five large pieces
1 rounded tsp coriander powder
½ tsp garam masala

Simple Spinach and Lentil Curry

This dish is so simple to make and is typical of home fare. It is the kind of dish that a mother makes for her family, is good for all ages and, despite the chillies, not really too spicy. Now a confession – it could be better. I could add some whole spices and fry an onion with the other tempering ingredients but generally, when at home, I would prefer to make something simple and healthy that tastes good rather than compete with heavier, restaurant fare. This curry is great with simple boiled rice, roti or even toast.

Place the lentils, water, ginger, chillies and turmeric in a pan, bring to a boil, then simmer over a moderate heat for 10 minutes. Stir in the tomatoes and cook for a further 20 minutes, then add the spinach and salt. Cook for another 10 minutes or so, until the lentils have started to break down and the curry comes together.

Meanwhile, heat the ghee, butter or oil in a small pan. Add the cumin seeds and garlic and allow the cumin seeds to redden and the garlic to start to brown. Stir in the coriander powder and garam masala, then pour the mixture into the pan of lentils. Cook for another minute and serve.

Serves 2

1 tbsp coconut or vegetable oil
$\frac{1}{2}$ tsp brown mustard seeds
$\frac{1}{2}$ tsp cumin seeds
$\frac{1}{2}$ small onion, peeled and finely chopped
1 tsp chopped fresh ginger
1 green chilli, left whole
200g fresh or frozen broad beans,
    podded and thawed if using frozen
salt, to taste
40g grated fresh coconut
8 fresh curry leaves, torn in half

Broad Bean Thoran

The British summer would somehow be incomplete without our tender, young, glistening broad beans. I love them as they are and generally prefer not to cook them, but they are perfect in this simple south Indian dish. I feel the need to grate fresh coconut to go with these beans to retain their inherent freshness and there is a simple, inexpensive gadget called a coconut scraper (see page 10) that helps me do this in minutes. If you are a coconut fan, it is well worth investing in one for beautiful, fluffy, sweet coconut flesh. This is a great side dish to accompany any summery meal or a quick protein snack, and you can even make it out of season using frozen beans.

Heat the oil in a pan, add the seeds and fry for 30 seconds. Add the onion, ginger and green chilli and cook for about 4 minutes over a lowish heat until the onions have softened.

Add the beans, salt and a splash of water and cook for 1 minute to warm through. Stir in the coconut and torn curry leaves, turn the heat down, cover, and cook for 2 minutes. Give the pan a stir and serve.

500ml water
100g split pigeon pea lentils (toovar
    dal), picked over and washed
½ tsp turmeric powder
1 tbsp ghee or vegetable oil
2–4 small dried red chillies, whole
    (I use birds eye chillies)
1 rounded tbsp chopped garlic
1 level tbsp dried mango powder, or
    to taste
salt, to taste
1 tbsp lemon juice, or to taste

Garlic and Chilli
Split Pigeon Pea Curry

This simple dish uses lots of store-cupboard ingredients. It is the arabiatta of the lentil world – spicy, garlicky and tart – using flavours that go really well with the savoury lentils. Leaving the chillies whole adds flavour without the heat. These lentils break down into a purée and as the dish cools it tends to firm up, so make sure the curry is not too thick before you take it off the heat.

Place the water and lentils in a saucepan and bring to a boil. Add the turmeric, cover and simmer over a low heat for about 20 minutes or until tender. Uncover and cook over a moderate heat for about 10 minutes until the lentils completely break down. If the lentils are too watery, increase the heat.

Heat the ghee or oil in a separate, small non-stick saucepan. Add the chillies and cook for a minute, then add the garlic. Cook over a moderate heat until the garlic is golden but not burned, then pour straight into the pan of lentils. Add the dried mango powder, salt and lemon juice to taste – the quantities of these depend on how tart your dried mango powder is. Serve hot. This curry solidifies as it cools, so add extra water if you are going to leave it to reheat later.

250g Bengal gram, well washed
2 bay leaves
1.2 litres water
$\frac{1}{2}$ tsp turmeric powder
1 heaped tsp coriander powder
1 tsp garam masala
salt, to taste
2–3 tsp sugar
2 tbsp mustard oil, unsalted butter
    or ghee
5 green cardamom pods
1 tsp cumin seeds
5 cloves
5cm shard of cinnamon
$\frac{1}{2}$ tsp brown mustard seeds
1–2 dried red chillies
3 heaped tbsp flaked or desiccated
    coconut, or $\frac{1}{4}$ small fresh coconut,
    flesh cut into small dice

Slightly Sweet Bengal Gram Lentil Curry

This popular Bengali dish is simple food and subtly spiced, as is most Bengali food. The lentils are meant to be thick, sweet and savoury and usually have raisins and coconut slivers to garnish, but I've omitted the raisins, simply because I'm not keen on fruit in curries. It is usually made with fresh coconut, but here I have changed it to dried, just because it is easier. It is normally eaten with the traditional luchi, a delicious deep-fried bread, but when I can't face the heaviness, naan or even a simple rice dish also goes really well with it.

Place the lentils, bay leaves, water and turmeric in a pan, bring to a boil and then simmer, covered for around 50–60 minutes or until soft. Add extra water, if necessary.

Stir in the coriander and garam masala, salt and sugar to taste. Cook until the lentils are completely soft and start to break up – I have an Indian wooden whisk that is ideal for this, but try anything that helps to break them up a little. You should be left with a thick lentily mass but with the actual lentils still discernible.

To serve, heat the oil or butter in a small pan (if using mustard oil, heat until smoking then cool and reheat) and fry the cardamom pods, cumin, cloves, cinnamon, mustard seeds and chillies for 30 seconds. Add the coconut and cook until it turns golden, then pour the mixture over the lentils. Stir in or leave to stir at the table.

Basmati Rice

Simple Pilaff

Spinach Pilaff

Lemon Rice

Wild Mushroom Pilaff

Creamy Rice and Lentils

BREAD and RICE

Coconut Rice

Simple
Layered
Flat
Breads

Roti

Naan

Basmati Rice

Serves 4

200g Basmati rice, cleaned in several
    washes of water until the water
    runs clear
365ml water
½ tsp lemon juice (optional)

Perfect Basmati rice is fluffy
and delicate. It has a wonderful
fragrance that is reminiscent of
an Indian meal, but, in reality,
many southern regions use their
own indigenous rice which is
thicker, shorter and nuttier. The
basic rule is one part rice to
one and a half parts water, but
the longer you soak it the less
water it needs – the moisture
from the soaked rice can
amount to more than you think.

Soak the rice in fresh, cold water
for 30 minutes for long and fluffy
grains.

Drain and tip into a thick-bottomed
pan for even cooking. Add the
water and bring to a good boil. Add
the lemon juice, if using, and give
it a good stir. Cover tightly, turn
the heat right down and cook for
7–8 minutes. Check after 7 minutes
– the grains should be cooked, but
if not, cover and test again after
another minute.

Turn off the heat and uncover.
Allow any excess moisture to
evaporate from the pan for
5 minutes, then fluff up with
a fork and serve.

Spinach Pilaff

Serves 3–4

2 tbsp oil
1 bay leaf
2 black cardamom pods
6 black peppercorns
1 tsp cumin seeds
1–2 green chillies, forked but left
    whole
1 small onion, peeled and chopped
300g cooked Basmati rice (see recipe
    on the left for method)
200g baby spinach leaves, wilted in a
    pan and puréed
salt, to taste
2–3 tsp lemon juice, or to taste

This pilaff works well as part of
any north Indian meal, but also
makes a good partner for grilled
chicken, simple lamb dishes or
chops, or even an assortment
of grilled vegetables. The spices
give it a wonderful rounded
flavour and the spinach provides
a velvety texture. The fact that
it is really good for us is almost
an afterthought. It is, needless
to say, great for children – my
daughter loves it (even with the
chilli) and I haven't yet needed
to hide the greenery!

Heat the oil in a large saucepan,
add the whole spices and green
chillies and cook for 20 seconds.
Add the onion and cook for about
4 minutes until translucent. Stir
in the rice, spinach and salt and
stir-fry to heat through. Just
before serving, add lemon juice
to taste.

Lemon Rice

Serves 2–3

2 tbsp vegetable oil
½ tsp mustard seeds
pinch of fenugreek seeds
¾ tsp split Bengal gram
¾ tsp split black gram
3 heaped tbsp peanuts, coarsely
    chopped (raw is best)
1–2 dried red chillies, left whole
1 tsp chopped ginger
¼ tsp turmeric powder
10 curry leaves, torn in half
salt, to taste
3 tbsp lemon juice, or to taste
300g cooked Basmati rice (see left)

This is a simple, fragrant rice
and makes the perfect partner
to any South Indian coconut
dishes as the tang of the lemon
contrasts beautifully with the
rich, sweet coconut. The
flavours are all reflective of
southern ingredients and this
vibrant dish is wonderful with
any of the fish, chicken or lamb
dishes in this book.

Heat the oil in a large non-stick
frying pan and add both seeds, the
lentils, raw peanuts (if using) and
chillies and stir-fry until the lentils
are light brown. Add the ginger,
turmeric powder, curry leaves and
salt and cook for 40 seconds.

Add the lemon juice and cook for
another minute. Add the rice and
roasted peanuts (if using instead
of raw peanuts). Stir-fry to heat
through, being careful not to break
up the grains too much. Serve hot.

Opposite: *Basmati Rice, left; Spinach
Pilaff, top right; Lemon Rice, bottom right.*

Coconut Rice

Serves 2

2 tbsp vegetable oil
½ tsp mustard seeds
½ tsp cumin seeds
2 dried red chillies, whole
1 tsp split Bengal gram
1 tsp split black gram
½ small onion, peeled and chopped
1 tsp finely chopped ginger
salt and freshly ground black pepper, to taste
2–3 tbsp roasted cashew nuts, broken up
10 curry leaves
250g cooked Basmati rice (see page 120 for method)
4 tbsp desiccated coconut, soak in water to cover before you cook (it will absorb most of the water)

This rice is from Andra Pradesh, a southern region known for its seafood and red chillies, and this subtly-flavoured recipe is a perfect foil for such ingredients. Fresh coconut has the best flavour and aroma, but you can use desiccated.

Heat the oil in a large non-stick frying pan, add the mustard seeds, cumin seeds, chillies and both lentils and fry until the latter start to colour. Add the onion and ginger and cook over a moderate heat for 4 minutes or until the onion is soft.

Add salt, pepper, cashews, curry leaves, rice and soaked coconut and stir-fry over a moderate heat until the rice is hot and all the flavours combined. Check the seasoning and serve.

Opposite: *Coconut Rice*

Creamy Rice and Lentils

Serves 1

35g Basmati rice
35g split and husked yellow mung lentils
1 rounded tsp ghee
½ tsp cumin seeds
½ small onion, peeled and chopped
1 green chilli, left whole (optional)
½ tsp chopped fresh ginger
½ clove of garlic, peeled and chopped
salt, to taste
½ tsp turmeric powder
400ml water
¼ tsp garam masala
¼ tsp freshly ground black pepper

This dish is easy to digest, nutritious and the first 'real' food babies eat. Eat with plain yoghurt and perhaps a pickle.

Wash the rice in water, then soak the rice and lentils in water for 30 minutes.

Heat the ghee in a medium-large non-stick saucepan. Add the cumin and fry for 20 seconds until colouring and aromatic. Add the onion and sauté for 4 minutes until soft. Add the chilli, ginger, garlic and salt and cook for 30 seconds, then add the drained rice and lentils, turmeric and water.

Bring to a boil for a few minutes, then simmer for 30 minutes until the rice and lentils are tender and breaking down to form a mass. Stir in the garam masala and pepper and adjust the seasoning.

The dish thickens as it cools so you may need to add a little water if you reheat.

Simple Pilaff

Serves 4

2 tbsp vegetable oil
1 tsp cumin seeds
1 small onion, peeled and thinly sliced
1 tsp garam masala
salt, to taste
200g Basmati or long-grain white rice, washed and soaked for 30 minutes
100g frozen peas
375ml water
1–2 tbsp lemon juice, or to taste

This is a quick and easy pilaff. Usually I add whole spices as it is, at heart, a spiced rice dish, but I realised it is better to encourage people to cook my food with a little compromise rather than not at all. So here is the result – a simple pilaff made with powdered spices.

Heat the oil a large non-stick saucepan. Add the cumin seeds and cook for about 30 seconds until fragrant. Add the onion and sauté for about 6 minutes until lightly caramelised. Add the garam masala and salt and cook, stirring, for another 20 seconds.

Stir in the drained rice and frozen peas, then add the water. Taste for seasoning. Bring to a boil, then cook, covered, on the lowest heat for 10 minutes. Check that the grains are tender; if not, leave to steam for another 2 minutes. Then remove the lid and allow any moisture to evaporate. Drizzle over the lemon juice and gently mix in with a fork, fluffing up the grains.

Serves 4–6

300g Basmati rice
200g good-quality wild mushrooms such
    as girolles, morels, ceps, oyster, etc
3 tbsp vegetable oil
1 small onion, peeled and chopped into
    1cm dice
large handful of raw cashew nuts, whole
5g garlic (approximately 2 cloves),
    peeled and finely chopped
salt, to taste
390ml water
1 tsp lemon juice, or to taste

Whole spices

1 tsp cumin seeds
2 bay leaves
1 large shard of cinnamon
2 black cardamom pods
6 green cardamom pods
6 black peppercorns
4 cloves

Wild Mushroom Pilaff

This is a special-occasion statement pilaff. It is a dish cooked either for those you love or for those you really want to love you. It is a dish that may send you on a treasure hunt for delicious wild mushrooms that will cost a little more than your standard button ones, but the results are well worth the extra effort. The delicate flavours of mushrooms and Basmati rice marry beautifully. The onion and cashew nuts add a hint of sweetness and texture to make the dish a sublime but subtle experience. Whole spices add a wonderfully rounded flavour but if you don't have any, leave them out and simply add one rounded teaspoon of garam masala instead (stir in with the mushrooms).

Wash the rice well and soak in cold water while you prepare the mushrooms. If using dried mushrooms, soak in boiling water for 20 minutes, then drain. Wash the morels well and wipe the other mushrooms clean with damp kitchen paper. Cut any large mushrooms into slices.

Heat the oil in a large, wide saucepan. Add the whole spices and cook for 20 seconds, then add the onion and cashew nuts. Fry for about 4–5 minutes until the onions are soft and browning at the edges. Add the mushrooms, garlic and salt and sauté over a high heat for 4–5 minutes.

Drain the rice and add to the pan of mushrooms with the water, bring to a good boil, then cover with a lid, lower the heat and cook for 10 minutes. Taste a grain of rice to check if it's cooked; if not, leave for another minute. Take off the heat, remove the lid and allow any excess moisture to evaporate. Gently stir in the lemon juice and taste and adjust the seasoning, if necessary.

Makes 6

150g chapatti flour, (or substitute half
    whole-wheat and half plain flour),
    plus extra for sprinkling
½ tsp salt
90–110ml milk or water
3 tbsp ghee or melted butter
1 tsp carom seeds

Simple Layered Flat Breads

These flat breads are so delicious and you can serve them with any North Indian meal. They are usually eaten with vegetarian food, such as lentil curries, simple vegetable dishes or scrambled eggs. When the breads are flavoured with dried mint, sesame seeds, poppy seeds, carom seeds or spring onions, they are often eaten with plain yoghurt and a pickle.

Mix together the flour and salt in a large bowl. Add the milk or water slowly until you have a soft, non-sticky dough (it might not require all the liquid). Knead for about 8–10 minutes, until the mixture has formed a smooth dough. Cover with a damp tea-towel and leave to rest for at least 10 minutes.

Divide the dough into six equal balls. Dust the balls lightly with flour. Take one and roll into a 15cm circle. Using the back of a spoon or your fingers, smear ¾ teaspoon of ghee or melted butter over the surface, sprinkle a little flour over it and a pinch of carom seeds.

Roll the bread up as you would for a tight Swiss roll, elongating the rope as you do by pulling the sides, for a long roll. Take one end of each piece of dough and coil it round on itself like rope. Press down with your fingers to flatten again. Dust with flour and roll out into a 12cm circle.

Heat a non-stick frying pan over a low heat. Place the dough onto the pan and turn the heat up a little. Once the top surface of the dough starts to dry out, turn it over. Take another ¾ teaspoon of ghee or butter and spread it over the surface. For a flaky finish, slash all over with the edge of the spoon you are using.

Once the underside has become golden, turn again and repeat with the ghee or butter and the spoon and cook until golden. Place on a plate covered with kitchen paper, cover the bread with more paper, and keep warm while you make the rest.

Makes 6

150g chapatti flour (or half whole-wheat
        and half plain flour)
salt (optional)
90–110ml water

Roti

Roti (or chapatti) is a basic whole-wheat flat bread which is eaten with almost every meal in northern India. These breads are soft, puff up when cooked and, if you use a gas cooker, lightly crisp on the underside. It is the easiest dough to make and doesn't require a bread machine. There is no real skill needed and when it comes to rolling the dough into a circle, the old adage applies – practice makes perfect. You can find chapatti flour in most large supermarkets, but you could also use equal quantities of whole-wheat and plain flour.

Sift the flour and salt, if using, into a bowl and make a well in the centre. Slowly drizzle in most of the water and, using your hand, draw the flour into the centre, mixing all the time. You may not need all the water as flour absorbs different amounts of water depending on its age and the moisture content in the air. It should be just slightly sticky.

Knead for 8–10 minutes. Then place in a bowl, cover with a damp tea-towel and leave for 30 minutes in a slightly warm area or at room temperature in the summer.

Divide the dough into six equal portions and roll into golfball-sized rounds; cover. Flour your work surface and rolling pin. Roll each ball into thin circles 12.5–15cm in diameter. The best way of doing this is to keep rolling in one direction, turning the dough a quarter of a circle each time to get a round shape.

Heat a tava or non-stick frying pan until quite hot. Toss the roti from one hand to the other to remove any excess flour, and place in the pan. Turn the heat down to moderate and cook until small bubbles appear on the underside, about 20–30 seconds, then turn. Cook this side until the base now has small dark beige spots.

The best way to puff up a cooked roti is to place it directly over an open flame (such as on a gas hob) using tongs. It will puff immediately, but leave for 3–5 seconds until dark spots appear, then turn and leave this side for a few seconds and place on a plate. Repeat with the rest. If you have an electric hob, press down gently on the cooked roti – as you press one area, the rest should puff up. Then tackle the next area – the roti should puff up all over.

Keep the bread warm by wrapping in a napkin or foil and placing in a low oven while you make the rest. You can reheat the roti, wrapped, in a medium oven.

250g plain flour
2 tsp sugar
$\frac{1}{2}$ tsp salt
$\frac{1}{2}$ tsp baking powder
110–130ml milk
2 tbsp vegetable oil
nigella seeds, poppy seeds, sesame
seeds, chopped garlic and fresh
coriander or a mixture of pumpkin
and sunflower seeds
1 tbsp butter, melted, for brushing

Naan

Everyone loves naan. It is the quintessential restaurant bread, made with plain rather than whole-wheat flour and is softer and more doughy than the other Indian flat breads. It is easy to make and the real thing is quite different from the supermarket version, which also tastes great but always seems to be a cross-breed between the original and good bread. Naan should be soft with a few crisp raised bits. Add a topping of your choice. I love nigella seeds the most, but even simple coriander and garlic make a great topping.

Sift together the flour, sugar, salt and baking powder. Mix together the milk and oil. Make a well in the centre of the dry ingredients and pour in the liquids.

Slowly mix together the dough by working outwards from the centre and incorporating the flour from the edges of the well to make a smooth, soft dough. Knead well for 8–10 minutes, adding a little flour if the dough is too sticky.

Place in an oiled bowl, cover with a damp tea-towel and leave for at least 1 hour in a warm place to double in size. When risen, punch out and form into five balls.

Preheat the grill to its highest setting and put a heavy baking sheet on the upper shelf.

Meanwhile, start to roll out the dough into teardrop or oval shapes, then gently prick all over with a fork. Sprinkle over the seed topping and press into the dough. Place the naans on the hot baking sheet and grill for 1–2 minutes or until there are brown spots on the surface. Brush with butter and serve hot.

Peshwari naan: to make this filled naan, pulse together 70g shelled pistachios, 35g raisins and $1\frac{1}{2}$ tsp caster sugar to make a coarse powder. Divide into five portions. Roll the naan into thick circles, fill each with one portion of the filling and pinch the dough around it to close. Roll out the naan again into teardrop or oval shapes. Sprinkle over 30g flaked almonds, then grill and serve as above.

Pomegranate
Raita

Tomato, Cucumber and Onion Raita

Green Chutney

Cucumber and Mint Raita

RAITAS
and
CHUTNEYS

Quick Tamarind Chutney

Pomegranate Raita

Serves 4

1 small pomegranate
400ml plain yoghurt
handful of chopped fresh coriander
    leaves and stalks
salt and freshly ground black pepper,
    to taste
$1/2 - 3/4$ tsp roasted cumin powder (cumin
    seeds dry-roasted until red and
    ground)
good pinch of red chilli powder, to taste

This is a refreshing, tangy raita, vivid in both colour and flavour, that brings a fresh sweetness to any Indian offering. These luscious fruits with jewel-like flesh come in different sizes so use your judgement on how much fruit to add. There is no right answer, so add as much or as little as you like, testing the flavour as you go along.

Lightly press down on the pomegranate and roll with your hands on a hard surface, applying a little pressure so that you help to release the seeds on all sides. Slice in half and, working over a bowl, tap the outside of the fruit with a wooden spoon. The seeds should tumble out. There may be too many for the raita so munch away.

Mix together the yoghurt, most of the pomegranate seeds and fresh coriander. Season with salt, lots of black pepper, the cumin and red chilli powder. Garnish with a handful of pomegranate seeds and a few coriander leaves.

Tomato, Cucumber and Onion Raita

Serves 4

1 tomato, diced
1 small red onion, peeled and diced
12.5cm piece of cucumber, peeled
    and diced
2 tbsp fresh chopped coriander leaves
    and stalks
400ml plain yoghurt
salt and freshly ground black pepper,
    to taste
$1/2 - 3/4$ tsp roasted cumin powder (cumin
    seeds dry-roasted until red and
    ground)
$1/4$ tsp red chilli powder

This is one of the most common raitas and the different textures and flavours make it a great accompaniment to any meal. Eat it as it is or serve it as a cooling summer dip with crudités or naan wedges.

Mix together the vegetables, coriander and yoghurt. Season with salt, plenty of black pepper and the roasted cumin powder.

Tip into a serving bowl, sprinkle over the chilli powder and serve.

Cucumber and Mint Raita

Serves 4

12.5cm cucumber
3 tbsp shredded fresh mint
400ml plain yoghurt
salt and freshly ground black pepper,
    to taste
$3/4$ tsp roasted cumin powder (seeds dry-
    roasted until red, then ground)
good pinch of red chilli powder

A great-tasting raita with the added bonus of having the combined cooling properties of mint, cucumber, yoghurt and cumin – a perfect way to counter heat in the food or in the air. Great with any meal or barbecue, or even just as a dip with naan, crudités or potato wedges.

Peel the cucumber, then coarsely grate and squeeze all the excess moisture from it.

Mix together the cucumber, mint and yoghurt. Stir in the seasoning and cumin powder. Sprinkle over the red chilli powder to serve.

Opposite: *Pomegranate Raita, left; Cucumber and Mint Raita, top right; Tomato, Cucumber and Onion Raita, bottom right.*

40g fresh mint leaves
10g fresh coriander leaves
½ clove of garlic, peeled
¼ small onion, peeled and chopped
1–2 green chillies, chopped (depending
    on how hot you like it)
12 raw pistachio nuts, shelled and
    chopped
¼ tsp dried mango powder or dried
    pomegranate powder
1 tbsp lemon juice, or to taste
salt, to taste
30ml water

Green Chutney

This is an all-purpose chutney, known as hara chutni. It is eaten with North Indian snacks, grilled tandoori dishes and even spread in sandwiches. Every home has their own recipe which might be as simple as herbs, seasoning and lemon juice. We often add dried mango powder but if you don't have any, add more lemon juice. Pistachios help bind the chutney which might otherwise become watery, but they can be omitted.

Simply purée all the ingredients for the chutney together in a food processor until smooth. Add as little water as possible, taste and add more lemon juice if necessary – it should be herby and lemony. Store in clean screw-top jars in the fridge; it will keep for a few days.

Serves 6–8 with snacks

3 tsp thick tamarind paste
4 tbsp brown or white sugar
$\frac{1}{2}$ tsp cumin seeds, dry roasted until
   fragrant and turning brown,
   then ground
$\frac{1}{4}$ – $\frac{1}{2}$ tsp freshly ground black pepper
60ml water

Quick Tamarind Chutney

In India the tamarind is mainly used to provide sourness to a dish and, in a curry, to help balance the sweetness from onions that often form its base. Other than that, it is really popular in this sweet, tangy and slightly spicy chutney. It is our version of ketchup and served in even smaller quantities. Its natural partners are many of the northern tea-time snacks, such as vegetable samosas. The strength of the tamarind paste varies slightly from brand to brand. I have used a well-known brand I found on my high street and noted that it contained salt so I had no need to add any. Check the ingredients of your paste and adjust the quantities of seasoning and sugar if necessary.

Put all the ingredients in a small saucepan, bring to a quick boil, then turn off the heat. Cool and serve judiciously.

This chutney can also be stored in screw-top jars in the fridge. It keeps well for weeks.

Nutty Saffron-flavoured Yoghurt

Steamed Yoghurt

Strawberry Lassi

Mango Smoothie

The Ultimate Masala Tea

Coconut Sweets

Lemon Lassi

Fennel Seed Drop-biscuits

Coconut and Jaggery Pancakes

DRINKS
and
DESSERTS

Sandesh

Kulfi

Charantais Melon Rasayana

Orange-scented Rice Creams

Jaggery-caramelised Walnuts

Serves 4

1 litre whole-milk yoghurt or
   500ml Greek-style yoghurt
2 tsp milk
$\frac{1}{2}$–$\frac{3}{4}$ tsp saffron strands
6–8 tbsp icing sugar, or to taste
   (depends on the tartness of
   the yoghurt)
$\frac{1}{4}$ tsp freshly ground green cardamom
   powder, or to taste
3 tbsp chopped unsalted pistachios
3 tbsp flaked or sliced almonds,
   lightly roasted
pomegranate seeds, to garnish
silver leaf, to garnish (optional)

Nutty Saffron-flavoured Yoghurt

This is a fantastic, vibrant dessert made with fresh yoghurt. It is an amalgam of thick yoghurt, summery, musky saffron and aromatic green cardamom, with nuts for added texture. I like to scatter a handful of pomegranate seeds over the top for a burst of colour and fruitiness. Yoghurt will vary in its degree of tartness depending on freshness, so add sugar according to taste. The potency of the saffron and cardamom powder also varies depending on freshness and quality, so use my measurements as a guide.

Line a large sieve with a double layer of good-quality kitchen paper. Place over a bowl and pour in the yoghurt. Refrigerate for as long as possible, at least 5–6 hours or until all the whey has drained off.

Heat the milk and crumble the saffron strands into the hot milk. Leave to infuse for 8–10 minutes, crushing the strands in the milk with the back of a spoon or your fingers.

Sift the sugar into the yoghurt and stir in along with the saffron milk, cardamom powder and half the nuts. Taste and adjust the sugar and cardamom powder if necessary. Chill and serve garnished with the remaining nuts, pomegranate seeds and silver leaf, if using.

Serves 4

500ml set natural yoghurt
95ml condensed milk
1$\frac{1}{2}$ tbsp raisins (optional)
20 pistachios, roughly chopped,
    or 2 tbsp flaked almonds, toasted
raspberries, to serve

Steamed Yoghurt

It really surprises me how much you can do with yoghurt and how every time I try something new, the results are always pleasantly surprising. The texture of this delicious dessert from Bengal is somewhere between a smooth panna cotta and a ricotta cheesecake. The longer you cook it, the grainier it becomes; this is not to say grainy is bad, some people prefer it one way, some the other. Raisins are optional – sometimes I like them in there, other times I just want some lovely seasonal fresh fruit. Most soft fruit goes really well with it.

Line a sieve with a double layer of kitchen paper and place over a large bowl. Pour in the yoghurt and allow the whey to drain off for at least 5 hours. If you wish, you can leave it, covered, in the fridge overnight, but be sure to drain away any liquid in the bowl after the first 2 hours.

Preheat the oven to 180°C/350°F/gas mark 4.

Whisk together the yoghurt, condensed milk and raisins (if using) until smooth. Divide the mixture between four small ramekins or oven-proof glasses. Cover each ramekin tightly with foil to prevent water getting in. Place them in a baking dish and pour in enough water to come a quarter of the way up the sides of the ramekins. Carefully place in the oven and cook for 30 minutes.

Cool the desserts in their pots and chill overnight. Either serve in their pots or turn out onto serving plates. Serve with the raspberries and sprinkle the nuts over the top.

Strawberry Lassi

Serves 2

200g ripe strawberries
200ml good-quality fresh plain yoghurt
1½–2 tbsp sugar, or to taste
ice cubes, to serve

Nothing speaks of the British summer quite like strawberries. It's the time when they are at their best – plump, sweet and juicy. And whenever the sun starts shining and the temperatures start to rise, the Indian in me craves a lassi. This is the drink that is taken in the rural areas by the farmers to help cool them down when working in their fields under a hot sun. It is traditionally made with buttermilk (the thin, slightly sour liquid that is the by-product of making butter) but it is much more convenient to cheat by using thinned-down plain yoghurt.

Blend the strawberries, yoghurt and sugar together until frothy. Pour into glasses and serve with the ice.

Mango Smoothie

Serves 2

2 Alphonso mangoes
300ml milk
2 tbsp sugar, or to taste
lots of ice cubes, to serve

This drink is creamy and fruity; it is the pure essence of mango. The Indian mango season spans the English summer and the king of the mango is the Alphonso – if you can find it, this is the one to buy. You can tell when it is ripe by its soft, yielding flesh and a sweet aroma. I have given approximate quantities as mangoes differ in size and sweetness so add and taste as you go along until you are happy. Chill the smoothies well before serving.

Standing the mango upright with the narrow end towards you, slice off both cheeks on the either side of the stone. Slice these in half lengthwise and remove the skin by peeling or slicing. Slice off the remaining sides of the stone as much as possible. Repeat with the second mango and put all the flesh and juices in a blender.

Add the milk and sugar and blend to a thick, smooth mass. Pour into glasses, each filled with ice cubes, and serve chilled.

Lemon Lassi

Serves 2

240ml good-quality fresh plain yoghurt
200ml water
3 tbsp sugar, or to taste
2–3 tsp lemon juice, or to taste
fine zest of 1½ small lemons
ice cubes, to serve
2 sprigs of fresh mint

This lassi is really refreshing and the fragrance of the lemon zest is pure summer. Good-quality, fresh yoghurt will stop this drink being too tart. I love it – it is better than lemonade and lighter than a milkshake or smoothie. Perfect for a healthy, outdoor life.

Blend together the yoghurt, water, sugar, lemon juice and zest until light and frothy. Adjust the sugar and lemon to taste. Pour into tall glasses filled with ice cubes and the mint and serve.

Opposite: *Mango Smoothie, left; Strawberry Lassi, right.*

Serves 4

1 litre full-fat milk
2 tbsp ground almonds
1 tbsp rice flour
5–6 tbsp sugar, or to taste
$\frac{1}{3}$ – $\frac{1}{2}$ tsp green cardamom powder,
  or to taste
2 tbsp chopped pistachios
2 tbsp flaked almonds

Kulfi

Kulfi is a traditional Indian ice-cream but made without cream and without eggs. At its simplest, it is a blend of reduced milk and sugar, flavoured with green cardamom powder. Restaurants normally add cream to the mixture. I have enriched my basic recipe by adding in some ground almonds and rice flour, but you can make a simpler version by doubling the quantity of milk and leaving out the almonds and flour. It does take a long time to make and does require some loving attention, but if you tend to hover around the kitchen, it's really easy to make. Just remember that you need to stir the mixture frequently to prevent the milk from catching on the base of the saucepan and burning.

Heat the milk in a wide, heavy-based pan over a low heat and bring to a boil. Then lower the heat and cook gently, stirring often. Place the ground almonds and flour in a small cup and once the milk is warm, stir in a little milk, make a thin paste and stir back into the pan with the sugar. Continue to cook gently as the milk needs to reduce by half – this takes about an hour. If a skin forms on the surface, just stir it back in.

Stir in the cardamom powder to taste. Cool completely, then decant into four kulfi moulds (I also know of it being set in polystyrene cups or normal freezerproof containers). If you have the time, 2 hours after it has been put into the freezer, take it out and give it a good whisk to break up any ice crystals.

Take the moulds out of the freezer 20 minutes before serving. Dip them briefly in hot water to loosen, then turn out onto serving plates. Sprinkle generously with the nuts.

**Makes 12 small pancakes
or 8 larger ones**

Pancakes

50g plain flour
pinch of salt
1 tbsp sugar
1 egg
150ml milk
25g unsalted butter, melted, plus
    extra for frying

Filling

80g jaggery (choose the darkest
    one you can find)
140g fresh coconut, grated
80g roasted salted cashew nuts,
    broken up

Coconut and Jaggery Pancakes

These filled pancakes are a lovely dessert, but can also be served as breakfast for the kids. I make fine, French-style crêpes as they are delicate and light and are perfect for desserts, rather than heavier American-style pancakes which would require more filling. I add salted cashews to this sweet filling as I think the salt just brings out the sweetness of the jaggery and coconut, but you can add plain roasted cashews or leave them out altogether. These pancakes freeze really well (separate them with greaseproof paper and wrap well). I have a small 12.5cm pancake pan which is the perfect dessert size, but use whatever size of pan you have and just be aware of quantities.

Sift the flour into a large bowl and add the salt and sugar. Make a well in the middle and crack in the egg, then pour in the melted butter. Using a whisk, slowly bring the sides of the flour into the well and mix until you have a smooth paste. Whisk in the milk and leave to rest for 30 minutes.

Meanwhile, mix together the ingredients for the filling.

Heat the pan until hot. Add a little butter and, when melted, pour in a ladleful or half a ladleful of batter, depending on the size of your pan. You want a thin covering. Turn the heat to medium and after 30 seconds or so, using a flat metal spatula, flip the pancake over. Cook the other side for another 15–20 seconds or until the base has a few brown spots.

Continue cooking the pancakes this way but without adding any more butter to the pan. Stack the pancakes on a plate, separating them with greaseproof paper.

When you are ready to eat, place 1–1½ heaped tablespoons of filling on one half of the pancake and fold. You can heat the filling in the pan if you wish, which will melt the jaggery, and if you heat the pancakes in the oven at the same time, this dessert will be great served with a scoop of vanilla ice cream.

Makes 12

1 litre full-fat milk
100–150ml yoghurt (depends how sour the yoghurt is), beaten
45g caster sugar
good pinch of saffron, powdered in a pestle and mortar with ¼ tsp sugar
½ tsp green cardamom powder (seeds taken out of the pods and ground)

Other flavouring ideas

1 tbsp rose water, or to taste
¾ tsp vanilla essence, or to taste
40g pistachio nuts, shelled and pounded to a rough purée (add an extra tbsp sugar to the cheese and add 1 tbsp milk)
good-quality chocolate powder, to taste
3 tbsp desiccated coconut, or to taste

To garnish

silver leaf, chopped pistachios, flaked almonds, saffron strands, flaked coconut or rose petals

Sandesh

To say that these little sweetmeats are made of fresh white cheese and sugar will not convey just how delicious they are. They are really moreish and when you know there is no added fat, you feel able to give in to temptation. These Bengali sweets are one of the most popular in a region renowned for its sweets and they are one of the few sweets still made at home in a culture that outsourced sweetmaking a long time ago.

Bring the milk to a boil in a pan set over a low heat. Once the milk starts to rise in the pan, stir in the yoghurt. The milk will curdle, leaving curd-like cheese floating in murky water. If it does not split, add some more yoghurt and leave for 20 seconds over the heat.

Line a sieve with muslin and place over a large bowl or saucepan. Strain the cheese into the lined sieve and discard the water. Run fresh tap water over the cheese to remove any sourness from the yoghurt. Twist the muslin around the cheese to make a tight ball and place it under a weight (I fill the pan with water and place it on top). Leave to drain for 20 minutes.

Place the cheese in a blender with the sugar and pulse three times to make a slightly grainy paste. Spoon the mixture into a cold non-stick frying pan and place over a low-moderate heat, stirring continuously for about 3–5 minutes. The mixture should leave the base of the pan and have the texture of soft dough. It will dry more as it cools. If in doubt, take a small bit and roll it into a small ball. It shouldn't crack and should hold its shape without being hard.

Now the basic mixture is ready. Add the saffron and the cardamom powder and roll into small walnut-sized balls. Garnish with silver leaf, chopped pistachios, flaked almonds, saffron strands, flaked coconut or rose petals, depending on the flavouring. Chill until ready to eat.

4½ tbsp rice flour
2 tbsp ground almonds
1 litre full-fat milk
4 tbsp sugar
½–¾ tsp green cardamom powder
1 heaped tsp grated orange rind, or
    to taste
10 pistachios, blanched, peeled and
    sliced
10 almonds, blanched, skinned and
    sliced, or flaked almonds
slices of blood orange, to garnish

Orange-scented Rice Creams

This is a popular, classic north Indian dessert, known as phirni. I have enlivened the recipe by adding orange zest which goes wonderfully with the warming cardamom. The rice flour helps the milk to set into an unctuous, aromatic mass with the ground almonds providing just enough bite. The creams are made a day in advance of serving so they have a chance to set and chill. Freshly ground cardamom has more flavour than shop-bought varieties so taste and adjust, if necessary. I set the creams in individual bowls or sometimes cocktail glasses for a little glamour, but you can use one large bowl and serve straight from there. For a richer version, replace some of the milk with double cream.

Mix the rice flour and ground almonds in 150ml of the milk to make a smooth paste. Heat the remaining milk in a pan on a medium heat, stirring constantly. As you bring it up to a simmer, stir in the rice-flour mixture.

Cook, stirring, over a medium heat for 10 minutes. Add the sugar, cardamom and orange rind and continue cooking for about 3–4 minutes until it reaches a semi-thick custard consistency. Pour into your serving dish of choice and chill. Garnish with the nuts and slices of orange before serving.

Serves 6

225g Charantais melon flesh (weighed without the skin), cut into small dice
225ml fresh or canned coconut milk
2 tbsp sugar, or to taste (depending on sweetness of melon)
seeds from $\frac{1}{2}$ a pomegranate
2 handfuls of crushed ice
handful of flaked almonds, lightly roasted in the oven until just changing colour

Charantais Melon Rasayana

This wonderful seasonal fruit is the stripy melon with the orange flesh. If you cannot find it, use cantaloupe or musk melon instead. Check it is ripe by sniffing one end – it should give off a fruity aroma. The Charantais melon is juicy and sweet and perfect in this refreshing south Indian-inspired dessert. The melon leaks into the creamy coconut and is uplifted with the pomegranate seeds.

Place the melon dice in a deep bowl. Using your fingers, crush them slightly so that they are no longer regular in shape and start to leak our their wonderful juice, but do not let them become mushy. Add the coconut milk and sugar and mix well. The colour should be a beautiful pale peach; you may want to give the melon another crush to assimilate the two. Stir in the pomegranate and chill until ready to serve.

Place a tablespoon of crushed ice in the bottom of the serving bowls and top with the rasayana. Sprinkle over the flaked almonds and serve cold.

Serves 3 to munch on or 5 as a garnish

100g jaggery, chopped or pounded into
smallish pieces
80g walnut halves

Jaggery-caramelised Walnuts

I love these little bites, which can also be used as a garnish for creamy Indian puddings or as a topping for yoghurt. They take just minutes to make. We already know that walnuts are good for us, but jaggery is amazing. It is a flavourful, completely unrefined sugar sold in blocks and renowned for its health properties. It is full of iron and other minerals and is known to help keep your lungs clean – in fact, many factories in Delhi give their workers a nugget every day to keep them healthy while working in a dusty environment. The best jaggery is quite dark and hard and needs to be chopped and pestle-and-mortared. It can be found in Indian shops, and although supermarkets have started to stock it, theirs is a softer, more watery version of the real thing. Either will work, but the darker jaggery has a more molasses-like flavour.

Place the jaggery in a saucepan and stir over a low-moderate heat to melt. Stir frequently to help it melt faster. When smooth, stir in the walnut halves. Stir to coat properly and cook for 1–2 minutes or until the jaggery has darkened in colour.

Place the walnuts individually on a sheet of baking paper or turn out onto an oiled plate. You have to work quickly as the jaggery will start to harden. If so, heat the pan a little to melt it again.

Store in an airtight container when cool.

The Ultimate Masala Tea

Makes 1 large cupful

350ml water
100ml milk
4 black peppercorns
10 green cardamom pods
good pinch of green fennel seeds
small shard of cinnamon
8g fresh ginger, peeled and roughly sliced
1 tea bag (I use a common black tea blend)
sugar, to taste
slightest pinch of salt (optional)

This is the ultimate cuppa. It is what women across India make when they have friends over. It offers solace and comfort and is invigorating and relaxing all at the same time. I drink a cup every morning without fail and no other tea does it for me anymore.

Heat the water, milk, spices and ginger in a pan. Once it comes to a boil, reduce the heat and cook over a low-moderate heat for 15 minutes. Be careful as the milk easily boils over. If this is about to happen, reduce the heat and take the pan off the heat for a few seconds.

Once reduced to a large cupful, add the tea bag and let it brew for 1 minute, or more if you like strong tea. Strain into your cup and add sugar or salt, to taste.

Opposite: *Masala Tea with Fennel Seed Drop-Biscuits*

Fennel Seed Drop-Biscuits

Makes 20

80g plain flour
70g caster sugar
2 tbsp skimmed milk powder
140ml milk
1 brown cardamom pod, seeds removed and pounded in a pestle and mortar
1½ tsp fennel seeds, ground
pinch of salt
1 tbsp ground almonds
2 tbsp melted butter
4 tbsp ghee or vegetable oil, for frying

These simple biscuits are part drop-scone, part biscuit. They are normally deep-fried, soaked in sugar syrup and served with thick, sweet milky desserts. I have added sugar to the batter and pan-fried them, keeping all the flavours but simplifying the cooking and lightening the dish.

Mix together the flour, sugar, powdered and whole milk, spices, salt, almonds and butter into a batter. Leave to rest for 10 minutes.

Heat the oil or ghee in a non-stick frying pan and drop small tablespoons of batter into the pan, keeping them separate. Fry over a moderate heat for about 1 minute on each side, until golden on both sides. Drain the biscuits on a plate lined with kitchen paper. They are best served straightaway while still warm, crisp on the edges and chewy on the inside.

Coconut Sweets

Makes 18–20

125g grated fresh coconut, or desiccated, if necessary
250ml full-fat milk
110g sugar
¼ tsp green cardamom seeds, ground
1 tbsp unsalted butter
2 tbsp chopped pistachios, to garnish

These sweet bites are easy to make. The only tricky bit is removing the coconut flesh, but you can use desiccated. Either buy a coconut scraper (see page 10), or break the coconut and carefully remove the flesh by getting a small paring knife under the brown skin and levering it out.

Place the coconut, milk and sugar in a non-stick pan and cook over a low heat for 20 minutes, stirring often. By now the mixture should come together in a lump. If you take a little bit in your fingers, it should be easy to roll and will set. If it is still too moist, cook for a couple more minutes and try again.

Add the cardamom and butter. Cook, stirring, for another 3 minutes. The coconut will colour slightly and come together really easily.

Make into little balls by rolling between your palms. Place on a plate and sprinkle over the chopped pistachios. If you can resist them, the sweets will keep well in the fridge, stored in an airtight container.

Glossary

As well as the more familiar English translations for ingredients, I've also given the Indian names which you may come across in Indian stores.

Spices

Asafoetida (heeng)
A really pungent powder that helps digestion and as such is added to many dishes that are hard to digest. Use the smallest pinch as it is very strong. If you don't have any, leave it out – it won't affect the dish too much.

Black/brown cardamom pod (badi elaichi)
These large woody pods look as though they are well past their sell-by date but have a wonderful and strong flavour when cooked. They are an important element in garam masala and pilaffs.

Black peppercorns (kali mirch)
Little needs to be said here, except that the taste and aroma of freshly ground peppercorns is far superior to store-bought powder.

Brown mustard seeds (rai)
These brown seeds are used a lot in India. It is to the south what cumin is to the north. It is also a key element in pickle making. When added to hot oil, the seeds will splutter, so it is good to have a cover handy to stop them popping out of the pan. Once cooked, they become almost nutty. When ground into a powder they provide a tart note to dishes and when ground into a paste they are the very essence of mustard.

Carom seeds/bishops weed (ajwain)
A small dark green seed that is reminiscent of thyme. It is quite strong so you only ever need to use a little. We often use it with fish and in some Indian breads. It is also an instantaneous cure for a stomach ache. Take half a teaspoonful with a pinch of salt and drink with hot water.

Chaat masala
A blend of spices that few Indians make at home. It is spicy and tart and Indians sprinkle it over many cooked foods and even drinks for a kick of flavour.

Cinnamon/cassia bark (dal chini)
Cassia bark is used more than cinnamon in India and has a smoother flavour. Use either sparingly as it has a big flavour and can overpower others. I add it in shards – any more and it will be too much.

Cloves (laung)
A strong spice that is most commonly used in garam masala. The natural oil in this is great for a toothache – bite down on the clove where it hurts and hold it there for as long as possible.

Coriander seeds and powder (sabut dhaniya)
Coriander seeds come from the flowers of the coriander plant. They are wonderfully mild and aromatic and are abundantly used. They have a subtle flavour but once you know what they taste like, you can always identify their presence. I often drink a coriander-seed tea after meals as it helps digestion and is cooling on the body. The seeds, when powdered, are used as a base for many masalas and it is probably the most used spice in my kitchen. Good-quality store-bought powder will be mossy green rather than brown.

Cumin seeds (jira)
This familiar spice is earthy when cooked in oil and nutty when dry roasted. It is an important spice in our cooking and adds a lovely rounded flavour. Great for digestion when made into a light warm tea.

Dried mango powder (amchur)
This ingredient is actually made from dried raw mangoes. It is tangy and we often sprinkle it on to cooked tandoori foods or fried potatoes instead of lemon juice or vinegar. It doesn't need cooking.

Fennel seeds/aniseeds (saunf)
A sweet, liquorish-like spice. They are often seen in the cuisine of Kashmir but also in the south. They are good for the stomach, and cooling and great for breast-feeding when infused in hot water. Also a natural breath freshener – chew on a few after a meal.

Fenugreek seeds (methr)
Strong, bitter seeds that have that familiar 'curry' flavour. Use very little at any time.

Garam masala
This famous blend is at its purest composed of the strong flavours of cloves, black cardamom, cinnamon and green cardamom. We add bay leaves, mace and black peppercorn to this. Many milder brands will add coriander and cumin seeds. This powder can be added towards the end of cooking for a real punch of aroma or closer to the beginning for a more rounded, subtle taste.

Green cardamom pod (chotti elaichi)
This is one of my favourite spices. It has a soft but powerful aroma and is used in sweet and savoury dishes and is essential in spicy tea. The seeds can be grund to make green cardamom powder.

Mace (javitri)
A wonderful flavour which goes very well with meat and chicken.

Nigella seeds (kalonji)
These delicate black seeds have a peppery flavour but without the bite.

Red chilli powder (lal mirch)
This is usually very hot and adds great colour to a dish but not much flavour.

Saffron (kesa)
Saffron is the dried stamen of the crocus flower. It is very expensive but a little goes a long way and it keeps well in the fridge. A lovely, musky flavour that works in both savoury and sweet dishes. Try to find long stamens.

Turmeric powder (haldi)
This vibrant powder is essential in Indian cooking. It is prized for its colour and its fantastic medicinal properties.

White poppy seeds (khus khus)
These are the same as the familiar dark poppy seeds but without the black husk. The skinless seeds have a smoother character.

Lentils

Bengal gram (channa dal)
The whole bean is similar to the chickpea but smaller and with a dark brown skin. Once skinned and split, the bean becomes a wonderful, earthy, yellow lentil.

Split and skinned black gram (urad dal)
This small, delicate lentil is used a lot in south Indian food for texture as it is sautéed to a nutty crunch without being pre-boiled.

Split and skinned mung bean (dhuli mung ki dal)
This small, pale yellow lentil is one of the easiest to digest and has a subtle, buttery flavour. At home, this is the lentil we eat most.

Split yellow pigeon pea lentil (toovar/arhar dal)
This lentil is often cooked until it completely breaks down to a smooth paste and is then spiced before being served. Wash well as it is usually coated in a film of oil to help preserve it.

Flours

Chapatti flour
A blend of whole-wheat and plain flour that is used to make our most common flatbreads. It can be found in Indian stores as well as many of the larger supermarkets. Substitute with equal quantities of plain and whole-wheat flour.

Gram flour (besan)
A key ingredient in Indian cookery and made from powdered Bengal gram. The Northern Indians use it to make batters, to bind marinades in tandoori foods, to flavour vegetables and also to make simple wheat-free breads. It has more protein than wheat. It can now be found in large supermarkets.

Rice flour
In India rice flour would be made by soaking the grains, drying them in the sun and then grinding them to a fine powder. This is used to add crispness to fried foods, to make dumplings in the south, to thicken curries and in the north to make a ground rice pudding. A delicate and fragrant flour that I love and use it as a thickener instead of cornflour.

Others

Buttermilk
A by-product of the butter-making process. It may seem like a tangy version of skimmed milk but, once flavoured, it is absolutely delicious and easier to digest than milk or yoghurt.

Curry leaves (kari patta)
These leaves are truly fragrant. They add a taste of the south to any dish they are added to.

Ghee (clarified butter)
Prized for its medicinal qualities in the East. It has a strong aroma and burns at a higher temperature than butter. See also page 12.

Jaggery (gur)
This is a completely unrefined sugar and probably the healthiest sugar around. It is made by boiling the natural sap from the date palm until it is hard and sets in a block. It is full of minerals and has a host of healthy properties. Workers in dusty Delhi factories are given little nuggets of jaggery to help keep their lungs clean. Buy the darkest you can find as they are less watery and have a more defined flavour.

Paneer
This traditional Indian cheese is made without rennet or bacterial culture (see page 26). It is similar to fresh farmer's cheese and is looks like solid ricotta. I think it is fabulous and is an important source of protein for Indian vegetarians.

Pilaff
A term used for any spiced and seasoned rice dish. It can be simple or contain any number of added ingredients.

Raita
A term used for yoghurt once it has had ingredients added to it. You can add cooked or raw, crunchy vegetables or even fruit to it. A wonderful summery dish that is great with any barbecues as well as full-on Indian meals.

Tamarind (imli)
The tamarind tree bears wonderful pods of fruit which are thick, fibrous and full of large seeds. But once softened and strained, the tamarind paste is a wonderful, tangy ingredient. It has a fruity, sour flavour and is used prolifically in the south, often to balance the sweetness of the coconut in their curries. The ready-made paste is available in the market but they all differ in strength so add to taste.

Tandoori cooking
A tandoor is a barrel-shaped clay oven and is so popular it is now eaten all over the world. The temperature in a tandoor can reach 500°F and gives dishes a barbecue-like flavour by searing it on the outside.

Index

Suppliers

There are so many shops and markets selling ingredients for Indian food that it would be impossible to guide you all to your local ones. By and large, we all know where we can find them so it is just a matter of making the time to go. For those who can't, here are some sites that will deliver all your ingredients to your door at the touch of a button.

Spiceworld.uk.com · The Asiancookshop.co.uk · Steenbergs.co.uk · Thespiceshop.co.uk

Spiceswarehouse.com · Pureindianspices.co.uk

Acknowledgements

Writing a book is always a production. Like an Indian wedding, it involves many key people without whom it wouldn't have been possible. I want to thank my husband for always believing in me and everything I do. To my sister, for always being so supportive and so generous with her time, filling in any gaps of loneliness in my daughter's life. To Heather, for being such a fantastic agent and ambassador. To Elly, for being so helpful and calm during the many periods of madness. To the powers-that-be in the BBC for giving me this fantastic opportunity and for such a wonderful experience. And last, but by no means least, to the team at Quadrille for succeeding so effortlessly in putting together this beautiful book in record time.